The Royal Horticultural Society

TREASURY
of GARDEN
WRITING

The Royal Horticultural Society

TREASURY
of GARDEN
WRITING

Selected by Charles Elliott

With illustrations from the
Royal Horticultural Society's Lindley Library

FRANCES LINCOLN

Frances Lincoln Limited
4 Torriano Mews
Torriano Avenue
London NW5 2RZ
www.franceslincoln.com

The Royal Horticultural Society
Treasury of Garden Writing
Copyright © Frances Lincoln Limited
2005

Text selected by Charles Elliott

Illustrations copyright © the Royal
Horticultural Society 2005
and printed under licence granted by
the Royal Horticultural Society,
Registered Charity number 222879.
Profits from the sale of this book are
an important contribution to the funds
raised by the Royal Horticultural
Society.

British Library
cataloguing-in-publication data
A catalogue record for this book is
available from the British Library

ISBN 0 7112 2522 2

Printed in China

9 8 7 6 5 4 3 2 1

CONTENTS

INTRODUCTION

Some pastimes just seem to breed exceptional writers. Angling is one such – who can resist the enchantment of Isaac Walton's *Compleat Angler*, in spite of knowing considerably more about fishmongers than fly rods? Gardening is surely another. In fact, it may be true to say that of all the avocations to which we dedicate our leisure (as well as time that might be spent in more practical pursuits) gardening is the richest and most varied source of good writing – profound, entertaining, instructive, and on many happy occasions, funny. The world would be a far poorer place if gardeners throughout history had not been inclined to lay down their trowels from time to time in favour of a pen, a typewriter, or a word processor.

The following selection of gardening prose extracts is necessarily both personal and inadequate. Personal because it covers only writers I particularly enjoy reading, including some who (like Jane Austen and Sir Walter Scott and Gustave Flaubert) are not strictly speaking garden writers at all, or only; inadequate because it merely skims the surface of a vast ocean of writing on creating gardens, admiring gardens, working in gardens, thinking about gardens, struggling to maintain gardens, and, of course, the plants that make the garden in the first place.

More than a hundred years ago, that great gardener Canon Henry Ellacombe (see page 98) remarked that by his calculation, no less than 10,000 books had already been written on his favourite subject. At least that many have been written since. And while some are frankly unnecessary, a few – quite a few, really – are treasures. If this small volume leads you to explore them, it will have done its job.

Charles Elliott

Henry Ward Beecher
'Pleasures of Horticulture'
Plain and Pleasant Talk about Fruits, Flowers and Farming,
1859

There is no writing so detestable as so-called *fine writing*. It is painted emptiness. We especially detest fine writing about rural affairs – all the senseless gabble about dew, and zephyrs, and stars, and sunrises – about flowers, and green trees, golden grain and lowing herds, etc. We always suspect a design upon our admiration, and take care not to admire. In short, *geoponical cant, and pastoral cant, and rural cant* in their length and breadth, are like the whole long catalogue of cants (not excepting the German Kant), intolerable. Now and then, however, somebody writes as though he knew something; and then a free and bold strain of commendation upon rural affairs is relishful.

I

GARDENING IN THE DAWN

In much of the earliest garden writing there is a sort of innocence and freshness, as if the writer has been agreeably stunned by the beauty and abundance around him. A rich and prominent Roman like Pliny the Younger might well have described his elegant villa and its garden in bragging tones; instead, he speaks with placid admiration, simply explaining how it is. Similarly, Sir Francis Bacon's detailed outline of the design and contents of a gentleman's garden is as intent to convey the human pleasures of sight and scent as it is to imply grandeur. Yet there is no lack of sophistication – witness William Lawson's worldly advice on hiring a gardener or Thomas Fuller's withering blast at the 'toolip'.

John Evelyn
Elysium Britannicum, 17th century

Whith what delight & satisfaction dos our Gardiner then behold some of these moddest & flowery Nymphs mantled in their greene scarfes, others halfe dressed (in the smocks of lawne) or indeede hardly borne! You would take some to be clad in white sattin or so much figured snow pinked, plaited, chambletted & embroiderd & chammare'd with gold; some have the resemblance of a soft mother of pearle, or a tender Emrauld; some like golden bells, silver, & of flexible Saphire, others present you with inammeled capps, pretty paniers, & boxes lined with crimson damaske with vasetts of chrystall achates & rubies of a gemmy luster. Their colours are pupurine, celestiall: incaradine, blushing Aurora, & virgine-white so innocent, so faire & smiling upon you sparkleling lively, orient, flaming & radiant: They peepe out of their buds as out of so many Eyes mealting and trickling into tears of joy & turne themselves into a hundred thousands formes & protean changes.

Pliny the Younger
Letter to Apollinaris, 1st century AD

My villa is so advantageously situated, that it commands a full view of all the country round; yet you approach it by so insensible a rise that you find yourself upon an eminence, without perceiving you ascended. Behind, but at a great distance, stand the Apennine Mountains. In the calmest days we are refreshed by the winds that blow from thence, but so spent, as it were, by the long tract of land they travel over, that they are entirely divested of all their strength and violence before they reach us. The exposition of the principal front of the house is full south, and seems to invite the afternoon sun in summer (but somewhat earlier in winter) into a spacious and well-proportioned portico, consisting of several members, particularly a porch built in the ancient manner. In the front of the portico is a sort of terrace, embellished with various figures and bounded with a box-hedge, from whence you descend by an easy slope, adorned with the representation of divers animals in box, answering alternately to each other, into a lawn overspread with the soft – I had almost said the liquid – Acanthus: this is surrounded by a walk enclosed with tonsile evergreens, shaped into a variety of forms. Beyond it is the Gestatio, laid out in the form of a circus, ornamented in the middle with box cut in numberless different figures, together with a plantation of shrubs, prevented by the shears from shooting up too high; the whole is fenced in by a wall covered by box, rising by different ranges to the top. On the outside of the wall lies a meadow that owes as many beauties to nature, as all I have been describing *within* does to art; at the end of which are several other meadows and fields interspersed with thickets. At the extremity of this portico stands a grand dining-room, which opens upon one end of the terrace; as from the windows there is a very extensive prospect over the meadows up into the country, from whence you

also have a view of the terrace and such parts of the house which project forward . . .

Between each plane-tree are planted box-trees, and behind these, bay-trees, which blend their shade with that of the planes. This plantation, forming a straight boundary on both sides of the hippodrome, bends at the farther end into a semicircle, which, being set round and sheltered with cypress-trees, varies the prospect, and casts a deeper gloom; while the inward circular walks (for there are several), enjoying an open exposure, are perfumed with roses, and correct, by a very pleasing contrast, the coolness of the shade with the warmth of the sun. Having passed through these several winding alleys, you enter a straight walk, which breaks out into a variety of others, divided by box-hedges. In one place you have a little meadow, in another the box is cut into a thousand different forms: sometimes into letters expressing the name of the master; sometimes that of the artificer; whilst here and there little obelisks rise, intermixed alternately with fruit-trees: when, on a sudden, in the midst of this elegant regularity, you are surprised with an imitation of the negligent beauties of rural nature: in the centre of which lies a spot surrounded with a knot of dwarf plane-trees.

Beyond these is a walk planted with the smooth and twining Acanthus, where the trees are also cut into a variety of names and shapes. At the upper end is an alcove of white marble, shaded by vines, supported by four small Carystian pillars. From this bench, the water, gushing through several little pipes, as if it were pressed out by the weight of the persons who repose themselves upon it, falls into a stone cistern underneath, from whence it is received into a fine polished marble basin, so artfully contrived that it is always full without ever overflowing.

When I sup here, this basin serves for a table, the larger sort of dishes being placed round the margin, while the smaller ones swim about in the form of little vessels and water-fowl. Corresponding to this, is a fountain which is incessantly emptying and filling; for the water, which it throws up a great height, falling back into it, is by means of two openings, returned as fast as it is received. Fronting the alcove (reflecting as great an ornament to it, as it borrows from it) stands a summer-house of exquisite marble, the doors whereof project and open into a green enclosure; as from its upper and lower windows the eye is presented with a variety of different verdures. Next to this is a little private recess (which, though it seems distinct, may be laid into the same room) furnished with a couch; and notwithstanding it has windows on every side, yet it enjoys a very agreeable gloominess, by means of a spreading vine which climbs to the top and entirely overshades it. Here you may recline and fancy yourself in a wood; with this difference only – that you are exposed to the weather . . .

Translated by William Melmoth

William Lawson
Of the Gardener and his Wages, 1660

Whosoever desireth and indevoureth to have a pleasant and profitable Orchard, must (if he be able) provide himself of a fruiterer, Religious, Honest, Skilfull in that faculty, and therewithall painefull. By Religious I meane (because many think Religion but a Fashion or Custom to goe to Church) maintaining, and cherishing things religious: as Schools of Learning, Churches, Tythes, Church goods and rights, and above all things, Gods word, and the Preachers thereof, so much as he is able, practising prayers, comfortable conferences, mutual instruction to edifie, almes, and other works of charity, and all out of a good conscience.

Honesty in a Gardener, will grace your Garden, and all your house, and help to stay unbridled Serving men, giving offence to none, nor calling your Name into Question by dishonest acts, nor infecting your family by evill counsel or example. For there is no plague so infectious as popery and knavery, he will not purloin your profit, nor hinder your pleasures.

Concerning his skill, he must not be a Sciolist, to make a shew or take in hand that which he cannot perform, especially in so weighty a thing as an Orchard: than the which there can be no human thing more excellent, either for pleasure or profit, as shall (God willing) be proved in the treatise following. And what an hindrance shall it be, not onely to the owner, but to the common good, that the unspeakable benefit of many hundred yeares shall be lost, by the audacious attempt of an unskilfull Arborist?

The Gardner had not need to be an idle or lazie Lubber, for so your Orchard, being a matter of such moment, will not prosper, there will ever be something to do. Weeds are alwayes growing, the great mother of all living Creatures, the Earth, is full of seeds, in her bowels, and any stirring gives them heat of Sunne, and being laid neer day, they grow: Moals work daily, though not alwaies alike: Winter hearbs at all times will grow (except in extream frost). In winter your trees and hearbs would be lightned of Snow, and your allies cleansed: drifts of Snow will set Deer, Hares, and Conies, and other noysome beasts over your walls and hedges into your Orchard. When Summer cloaths your borders with green and peckled colours, your Gardner must dress his hedges, and antick works: watch his Bees, and hive them: Distil his Roses and other Hearbs. Now begin Summer fruits to ripe, and crave your hand to pull them. If he have a Garden (as he must needs) to keep, you must needs allow him good helpe, to end his labours which are endlesse; for no one man is sufficient for these things.

Such a Gardner as will conscionably, quietly and patiently, travel in your Orchard, God shall Crown the labours of his hands with joyfulnesse, and make the clouds drop fatnesse upon your trees; he will provoke your love, and earn his wages, and fees belonging to his place. The house being served, fallen fruit, superfluity of hearbs, and flowers, seeds, grasses, Sets, and besides all other of that fruit which your bountifull hand shall reward him withall, will much augment his wages, and the profit of your Bees will pay you back again.

If you be not able, nor willing to hire a Gardner, keep your profits to yourself, but then you must take all the pains; and for that purpose (if you want this faculty) to instruct you, have I undertaken these labours, and gathered these Rules, but chiefly respecting my Countries good.

A

NEVV ORCHARD
AND GARDEN

OR

The beſt way for planting, grafting, and to make any ground good, for a rich Orchard: Particularly in the North, and generally for the whole kingdome of *England*, as in nature, reaſon, ſituation, and all probabilitie, may and doth appeare.

With the Country Houſewifes Garden for hearbes of common vſe their vertues, ſeaſons, profits, ornaments, varietie of knots, models for trees, and plots for the beſt ordering of Grounds and Walkes.

AS ALSO

The Husbandry of Bees, with their ſeuerall vſes and annoyances all being the experience of 48. yeares labour, and now the ſecond time corrected and much enlarged, by *William Lawſon.*

Whereunto is newly added the Art of propagating Plants, with the true ordering of all manner of Fruits, in their gathering, carring home, & preſeruation.

Skill and paines bring fruitfull gaines

Nemo ſibi natus.

Sir William Temple
'Of the Gardens of Epicurus: or Of Gardening in the Year 1685', 1692

What I have said, of the best forms of gardens, is meant only of such as are in some sort regular; for there may be other forms wholly irregular that may, for aught I know, have more beauty than any of the others; but they must owe it to some extraordinary dispositions of nature in the seat, or some great race of fancy or judgment in the contrivance, which may reduce many disagreeing parts into some figure, which shall yet, upon the whole, be very agreeable. Something of this I have seen in some places, but heard more of it from others who have lived much among the Chineses; a people whose way of thinking seems to lie as wide of ours in Europe, as their country does. Among us, the beauty of building and planting is placed chiefly in some certain proportions, symmetries, or uniformities; our walks and our trees ranged so as to answer one another, and at exact distances. The Chineses scorn this way of planting, and say, a boy, that can tell an hundred, may plant walks of trees in straight lines, and over-against one another, and to what length and extent he pleases. But their greatest reach of imagination is employed in contriving figures, where the beauty shall be great, and strike the eye, but without any order or disposition of parts that shall be commonly or easily observed: and, though we have hardly any notion of this sort of beauty, yet they have a particular word to express it, and, where they find it hit their eye at first sight, they say the *sharawadgi* is fine or is admirable, or any such expression of esteem. And whoever observes the work upon the best India gowns, or the painting upon their best screens or purcellans, will find their beauty is all of this kind (that is) without order. But I should hardly advise any of these attempts in the figure of gardens among us; they are adventures of too hard achievement for any common hands; and, though there may be more honour if they succeed well, yet there is more dishonour if they fail, and it is twenty to one they will; whereas, in regular figures, it is hard to make any great and remarkable faults.

What I have said of gardening is perhaps enough for any Gentleman to know, so as to make no great faults, nor be much imposed upon in the designs of that kind, which I think ought to be applauded and encouraged in all countries; that and building being a sort of creation, that raise beautiful fabrics and figures out of nothing, that make the convenience and pleasure of all private habitations, that employ many hands, and circulate much money among the poorer sort and artisans, that are a public service to one's country, by the example as well as effect, which adorn the scene, improve the earth and even the air itself in some degree. The rest that belongs to this subject must be a gardener's part; upon whose skill, diligence, and care, the beauty of the grounds and excellence of the fruits will much depend. Though if the soil and sorts be well chosen, well suited, and disposed to the walls, the ignorance or carelessness of the servants can hardly leave the master disappointed.

Sir Francis Bacon
'Of Gardens'
Essays Civil and Moral, 1625

God Almighty planted a garden. And indeed it is the purest of human pleasures. It is the greatest refreshment to the spirits of man; without which, buildings and palaces are but gross handiworks; and a man shall ever see, that when ages grow to civility and elegancy, men come to build stately sooner than to garden finely; as if gardening were the greater perfection. I do hold it, in the royal ordering of gardens, there ought to be gardens, for all the months in the year; in which severally things of beauty may be then in season. . . .

And because the breath of flowers is far sweeter in the air (where it comes and goes like the warbling of music) than in the hand, therefore nothing is more fit for that delight, than to know what be the flowers and plants that do best perfume the air. Roses, damask and red, are fast flowers of their smells; so that you may walk by a whole row of them, and find nothing of their sweetness; yea though it be in a morning's dew. Bays likewise yield no smell as they grow. Rosemary little; nor sweet marjoram. That which above all others yields the sweetest smell in the air is the violet, specially the white double violet, which comes twice a year; about the middle of April, and about Bartholomew-tide. Next to that is the musk-rose. Then the strawberry-leaves dying, which [yield] a most excellent cordial smell. Then the flower of vines; it is a little dust, like the dust of a bent, which grows

upon the cluster in the first coming forth. Then sweet-briar. Then wall-flowers, which are very delightful to be set under a parlour or lower chamber window. Then pinks and gilliflowers, especially the matted pink and clove gilliflower. Then the flowers of the lime-tree. Then the honeysuckles, so they be somewhat afar off. Of beanflowers I speak not, because they are field flowers. But those which perfume the air most delightfully, not passed by as the rest, but being trodden upon and crushed, are three; that is, burnet, wild-thyme, and watermints. Therefore you are to set whole alleys of them, to have the pleasure when you walk or tread.

For gardens (speaking of those which are indeed princelike, as we have done of buildings), the contents ought not well to be under thirty acres of ground; and to be divided into three parts; a green in the entrance; a heath or desert in the going forth; and the main garden in the midst; besides alleys on both sides. And I like well that four acres of ground be assigned to the green; six to the heath; four and four to either side; and twelve to the main garden. The green hath two pleasures: the one, because nothing

is more pleasant to the eye than green grass kept finely shorn; the other, because it will give you a fair alley in the midst, by which you may go in front upon a stately hedge, which is to enclose the garden. But because the alley will be long, and, in great heat of the year or day, you ought not to buy the shade in the garden, by going in the sun through the green, therefore you are, of either side the green, to plant a covert alley upon carpenter's work, about twelve foot in height, by which you may go in shade into the garden. As for the making of knots or figures, with divers coloured earths, that they may lie under the windows of the house on that side which the garden stands, they be but toys; you may see as good sights, many times, in tarts. The garden is best to be square, encompassed on all the four sides with a stately arched hedge. . . .

For the ordering of the ground, within the great hedge, I leave it to variety of device; advising nevertheless, that whatsoever form you cast it into, first, it be not too busy, or full of work. Wherein I, for my part, do not like images cut out in juniper or other garden stuff; they be for children. Little low hedges, round, like welts, with some pretty pyramids, I like well;

and in some places, fair columns upon frames of carpenter's work. I would also have the alleys, spacious and fair. . . .

For fountains, they are a great beauty and refreshment; but pools mar all, and make the garden unwholesome, and full of flies and frogs. Fountains I intend to be of two natures: the one that sprinkleth or spouteth water; the other a fair receipt of water, of some thirty or forty foot square, but without fish, or slime, or mud. For the first, the ornaments of images gilt, or of marble, which are in use, do well: but the main matter is so to convey the water, as it never stay . . .

For the heath, which was the third part of our plot, I wish it to be framed, as much as may be, to a natural wildness. Trees I would have none in it, but some thickets made only of sweet-briar and honeysuckle, and some wild vine amongst; and the ground set with violets, strawberries, and primroses. For these are sweet, and prosper in the shade. And these to be in the heath, here and there, not in any order. I like also little heaps, in the nature of mole-hills (such as are in wild heaths), to be set, some with wild thyme; some with pinks; some with germander, that gives a good flower to the eye; some with periwinkle; some with violets; some with strawberries; some with cowslips; some with daisies; some with red roses; some with lilium convallium; some with sweet-williams red; some with bear's-foot: and the like low flowers, being withal sweet and sightly. Part of which heaps, are to be with standards of little bushes pricked upon their top, and part without. The standards to be roses; juniper; hory; berberries (but here and there, because of the smell of their blossoms); red currants; gooseberries; rosemary; bays; sweet-briar; and such like. But these standards to be kept with cutting, that they grow not out of course. . . .

For the main garden, I do not deny, but there should be some fair alleys ranged on both sides, with fruit-trees; and some pretty tufts of fruit-trees; and arbors with seats, set in some decent order; but these to be by no means set too thick; but to leave the main garden so as it be not close, but the air open and free. For as for shade, I would have you rest upon the alleys of the side grounds, there to walk, if you be disposed, in the heat of the year or day; but to make account, that the main garden is for the more temperate parts of the year; and in the heat of summer, for the morning and the evening, or overcast days.

For aviaries, I like them not, except they be of that largeness as they may be turfed, and have living plants and bushes set in them; that the birds may have more scope, and natural nestling, and that no foulness appear in the floor of the aviary. So I have made a platform of a princely garden, partly by precept, partly by drawing, not a model, but some general lines of it; and in this I have spared for no cost. But it is nothing for great princes, that for the most part taking advice with workmen, with no less cost set their things together; and sometimes add statuas and such things for state and magnificence, but nothing to the true pleasure of a garden.

Sir Thomas Browne
The Garden of Cyrus, 1658

You have wisely ordered your vegetable delights, beyond the reach of exception. The Turks who passt their dayes in Gardens here, will have Gardens also hereafter, and delighting in Flowers on earth, must have Lilies and Roses in Heaven. In Garden Delights 'tis not easie to hold a Mediocrity; that insinuating pleasure is seldome without some extremity. The Antients venially delighted in flourishing Gardens; Many were Florists that knew not the true use of a Flower; and in Plinies dayes none had directly treated of that Subject. Some commendably affected Plantations of venemous Vegetables, some confined their delights unto single plants, and Cato seemed to dote upon Cabbadge; While the Ingenuous delight of Tulipists, stands saluted with hard language, even by their own Professors. . . . That we conjoyn these parts of different Subjects, or that this should succeed the other; Your judgement will admit without impute of incongruity; Since the delightfull World comes after death, and Paradise succeeds the Grave. Since the verdant state of things is the Symbole of the Resurrection, and to flourish in the state of Glory, we must first be sown in corruption. Beside the antient practise of Noble Persons, to conclude in Garden-Graves, and Urnes themselves of old, to be wrapt up in flowers and garlands.

Thomas Fuller
Antheologia, 1660

There is lately a *Flower* (shal I call it so? in courtesie I will tearme it so, though it deserve not the appellation) a *Toolip*, which hath engrafted the love and affections of most people unto it; and what is this Toolip? a well complexion'd stink, an ill favour wrapt up in pleasant colours; as for the use thereof in *Physick*, no *Physitian* hath honoured it yet with the mention, nor with a *Greek*, or Latin name, so inconsiderable hath it hitherto been accompted; and yet this is that which filleth all Gardens, hundred of pounds being given for the root thereof, whilst I the *Rose*, am neglected and contemned, and conceived beneath the honour of noble hands, and fit only to grow in the gardens of Yeomen. I trust the remainder to your apprehensions, to make out that which grief for such undeserved injuries will not suffer me to expresse.

Robert Laneham
Letter describing the pageants at Kenilworth Castle during the visit of Queen Elizabeth I in 1575

Unto this, his Honor's (the Earl of Leicester's) exquisite appointment of a beautiful garden, an acre or more in quantity, that lieth on the north there: Whereon hard all along by the Castle wall is reared a pleasant terrace, ten feet high, and twelve feet broad, even under foot, and fresh of fine grass; as is also the side thereof towards the garden: In which, by sundry equal distances, with obelisks and spheres, and white bears, all of stone upon their curious bases, by goodly shew were set; To these, two fine arbours redolent by sweet trees and flowers, at each end one, the garden plot under that, with fair alleys, green by grass, even voided from the borders on both sides, and some (for change) with sand, not light, or too soft, or soily by dust, but smooth and firm, pleasant to walk on, as a sea-shore when the water is availed. Then, much gracified by due proportion of four even quarters; in the midst of each, upon a base of two feet square, and high, seemly bordered of itself, a square pilaster rising pyramidically fifteen feet high. Symmetrically pierced through from a foot beneath to two feet of the top: whereupon, for a Capital, an orb of ten inches thick; every one of these, with its base, from the ground to the top, of one whole piece; hewn out of hard porphyry, and with great art and heed (think me) thither conveyed and there erected. Where, further also, by great cast and cost, the sweetness of savour on all sides, made so respirant from the redolent plants, and

fragrant herbs and flowers, in form, colour, and quantity so deliciously variant; and fruit-trees bedecked with apples, pears, and ripe cherries. . . .

A garden then so appointed, as wherein aloft upon sweet shadowed walk of terrace, in heat of summer to feel the pleasant whisking wind above, or delectable coolness of the fountain-spring beneath; to taste of delicious strawberries, cherries, and other fruits, even from their stalks; to smell such fragrancy of sweet odours, breathing from the plants, herbs, and flowers; to hear such natural melodious music and tunes of birds; to have in eye for mirth sometime these underspringing streams; then, the woods, the waters (for both pool and chase were hard at hand in sight), the deer, the people (that out of the East arbour in the base Court, also at hand in view), the fruit-trees, the plants, the herbs, the flowers, the change in colours, the birds flittering, the fountain streaming, the fish swimming, all in such delectable variety, order, and dignity; whereby, at one moment, in one place, at hand, without travel, to have so full fruition of so many God's blessings, by entire delight unto all senses (if all can take) at once; for etymon of the word worthy to be called Paradise: and though not so goodly as Paradise, for want of the fair rivers, yet better a great deal by the lack of so unhappy a tree. Argument most certain of a right noble mind, that in this sort could have thus all contrived.

John Parkinson
Paradisi in Sole Paradisus Terrestris, 1629

Your knot or beds being prepared fitly, as before is declared, you may place and order your roots therein thus: Eyther many rootes of one kinde set together in a round or cluster, or longwise crosse a bed one by another, whereby the beauty of many flowers of one kinde being together, may make a fair shew well pleasing to many; or else you may plant one or two in a place dispersedly over the whole knot, or in a proportion or diameter one place answering another of the knot, as your store will suffer you, or your knot permit: Or you may also mingle these rootes in their planting many divers sorts together, that they may give the more glorious show when they arte in flower; and that you may so doe, you must first observe the severall kindes of them, which doe flower at one and the same time, and then to place them in such order and so neare one unto another, that their flowers appearing together of severall colours, will cause the more admiration in the beholders: as thus, the Vernall Crocus or Saffron-flowers of the Spring, white, purple, yellow, and stript, with some Vernall Colchicum or Medow Saffron among them, some Deus Caninus or Doggesteeth, and some of the small early Leucoium or Bulbous Violet, all planted in some proportion as neare one unto another as is fit for them, will give such a grace to the Garden, that the place will seeme like a peece of tapestry of many glorious colours, to encrease every one's delight: Or else many of one sort together as blew,

white and bluish Grapes flowers in the same manner intermingled, doe make a marvellous delectable shew, especially because all of them rise almost to an equal height, which causeth the greater grace, as well neare hand as far of. The like order may be kept with many other things, as the Hepatica, white, blew, purple, and red set or sowne together, will make many to beleeve that one roote doth bear all those colours: But above and beyond all others, the Tulipas may be so matched, one colour answering and setting of another, that the place where they stand may resemble a peece of curious needleworke, or peece of painting: and I have knowne in a Garden, the Master as much commended for this artificiall forme in placing the colours of Tulipas, as for the goodnesse of his flowers, or any other thing. The divers sorts and colours of Anemones or Winde-flowers may be so ordered likewise, which are oft very beautifull, to have the severall varieties place one very neare unto another, that their severall colours appearing in one place will be a very great grace in a Garden, or if they be dispersed among the other sorts of flowers, they will make a glorious shew. Another order in planting you may observe: which is this, That those plants that grow low, as the Aconitum Hyemale or Winterwolves bane, the Vernall Crocus or Saffron-flowers of divers sorts, the little early Leucoium or Bulbous Violet, and some such other as rise not up very high, as also some Anemones may be very well placed somewhat neare or about your Martagons, Lillies, or Crownes Imperiall, both because these little plants will flower earlier than they, and so will be gone and past, before the other greater plants will rise up to any height to hinder them; which is a way may well be admitted in those Gardens that are small, to save roome, and to place things to the most advantage.

II

WITS AND LANDSCAPERS

The eighteenth century was famously involved with landscape gardening. At least it's fair to say that much of the garden writing of the era concerned itself with design, usually on a large scale, with proponents of sweeping lawns and strategically placed copses at frequent war with those in favour of the 'picturesque' or other departures from the formality of earlier times. In the eyes of Horace Walpole the key element was the ha-ha, to Sir Walter Scott what mattered were trees, while to Oliver Goldsmith the answer was Chinese spontaneity (though he had never been anywhere near China). All of which was marvellous ammunition for the satirists. See Jane Austen and Thomas Love Peacock – and my favourite, Flaubert.

Horace Walpole
On Modern Gardening, 1771

At that moment appeared Kent, painter enough to taste the charms of landscape, bold and opinionative enough to dare and to dictate, and born with a genius to strike out a great system from the twilight of imperfect essays. He leaped the fence, and saw that all nature was a garden. He felt the delicious contrast of hill and valley changing imperceptibly into each other, tasted the beauty of the gentle swell, or concave scoop, and remarked how loose groves crowned an easy eminence with happy ornament, and while they called in the distant view between their graceful stems, removed and extended the perspective by delusive comparison.

Thus the pencil of his imagination bestowed all the arts of landscape on the scenes he handled. The great principles on which he worked were perspective, and light and shade. Groupes of trees broke too uniform or too extensive a lawn; evergreens and woods were opposed to the glare of the champain, and where the view was less fortunate, or so much exposed as to be beheld at once, he blotted out some parts by thick shades, to divide it into variety, or to make the richest scene more enchanting by reserving it to a farther advance of the spectator's step. Thus, selecting favourite objects, and veiling deformities by screens of plantation; sometimes allowing the rudest waste to add its foil to the richest theatre, he realized the compositions of the greatest masters in painting. Where objects were wanting to animate his horizon, his taste as an architect could bestow immediate termination. His buildings, his seats, his temples, were more the works of his pencil than of his compasses. We owe the restoration of Greece and the diffusion of architecture to his skill in landscape.

But of all the beauties he added to the face of this beautiful country, none surpassed his management of water. Adieu to canals, circular basons, and cascades tumbling down marble steps, that last absurd magnificence of Italian and French villas. The forced elevation of cataracts was no more. The gentle stream was taught to serpentize seemingly at its pleasure, and where discontinued by different levels, its course appeared to be concealed by thickets properly interspersed, and glittered again at a distance where it might be supposed naturally to arrive. Its borders were smoothed, but preserved their waving irregularity. A few trees scattered here and there on its edges sprinkled the tame bank that accompanied its mæanders; and when it disappeared among the hills, shades descending from the heights leaned towards its progress, and framed the distant point of light under which it was lost, as it turned aside to either hand of the blue horizon.

Thus dealing in none but the colours of nature, and catching its most favourable features, men saw a new creation opening before their eyes. The living landscape was chastened or polished, not transformed. Freedom was given to the forms of trees; they extended their branches unrestricted, and where any eminent oak, or master beech had escaped maiming and survived the forest, bush and bramble was removed, and all its honours were restored to distinguish and shade the plain. Where the united plumage of an ancient wood extended wide its undulating canopy, and stood venerable in its darkness, Kent thinned the foremost ranks, and

left but so many detached and scattered trees, as softened the approach of gloom and blended a chequered light with the thus lengthened shadows of the remaining columns.

Jane Austen
Mansfield Park, 1814

She must try to find amusement in what was passing at the upper end of the table, and in observing Mr. Rushworth, who was now making his appearance at Mansfield for the first time since the Crawfords' arrival. He had been visiting a friend in the neighbouring county, and that friend having recently had his grounds laid out by an improver, Mr. Rushworth was returned with his head full of the subject, and very eager to be improving his own place in the same way; and though not saying much to the purpose, could talk of nothing else. The subject had been already handled in the drawing-room; it was revived in the dining-parlour. Miss Bertram's attention and opinion was evidently his chief aim; and though her deportment showed rather conscious superiority than any solicitude to oblige him, the mention of Sotherton Court, and the ideas attached to it, gave her a feeling of complacency, which prevented her from being very ungracious.

'I wish you could see Compton,' said he; 'it is the most complete thing! I never saw a place so altered in my life. I told Smith I did not know where I was. The approach *now*, is one of the finest things in the country: you see the house in the most surprising manner. I declare, when I got back to Sotherton yesterday, it looked like a prison – quite a dismal old prison.'

'Oh, for shame!' cried Mrs. Norris. 'A prison indeed? Sotherton Court is the noblest old place in the world.'

'It wants improvement, ma'am, beyond anything. I never saw a place that wanted so much improvement in my life; and it is so forlorn that I do not know what can be done with it.'

'No wonder that Mr. Rushworth should think so at present,' said Mrs. Grant to Mrs. Norris, with a smile; 'but depend upon it, Sotherton will have every improvement in time which his heart can desire.'

'I must try to do something with it,' said Mr. Rushworth, 'but I do not know what. I hope I shall have some good friend to help me.'

'Your best friend upon such an occasion,' said Miss Bertram calmly, 'would be Mr. Repton, I imagine.'

'That is what I was thinking of. As he has done so well by Smith, I think I had better have him at once. His terms are five guineas a day.'

'Well, and if they were *ten*,' cried Mrs. Norris, 'I am sure *you* need not regard it. The expense need not be any impediment. If I were you, I should not think of the expense. I would have everything done in the best style, and made as nice as possible. Such a place as Sotherton Court deserves everything that taste and money can do. You have space to work upon there, and grounds that will well reward you. For my own part, if I had anything within the fiftieth part of the size of Sotherton, I should be always planting and improving, for naturally I am excessively fond of it. It would be too ridiculous for me to attempt anything where I am now, with my little half acre. It would be quite a burlesque. But if I had more room, I should take a prodigious delight in improving and planting. We did a vast deal in that way at the Parsonage: we made it quite a different place from what it was when we first had it. You young ones do not remember much about it, perhaps; but if dear Sir Thomas were here, he could tell you what improvements we made: and a great deal more would have been done, but for poor Mr. Norris's sad state of health. He could hardly ever get out, poor man, to enjoy anything, and *that* disheartened me from doing several things that Sir Thomas and I used to talk of. If it had not been for *that*, we should have carried on the garden wall, and made the plantation to shut out the churchyard, just as Dr. Grant has done. We were always doing something as it was. It was only the spring twelvemonth before Mr. Norris's death that we put in the apricot against the stable wall, which is now grown such a noble tree, and getting to such perfection, sir,' addressing herself then to Dr. Grant.

'The tree thrives well, beyond a doubt, madam,' replied Dr. Grant. 'The soil is good; and I never pass it without regretting that the fruit should be so little worth the trouble of gathering.'

'Sir, it is a Moor Park, we bought it as a Moor Park, and it cost us – that is, it was a present from Sir Thomas, but I saw the bill – and I know it cost seven shillings, and was charged as a Moor Park.'

'You were imposed on, ma'am,' replied Dr. Grant: 'these potatoes have as much the flavour of a Moor Park apricot as the fruit from that tree. It is an insipid fruit at the best; but a good apricot is eatable, which none from my garden are.'

'The truth is, ma'am,' said Mrs. Grant, pretending to whisper across the table to Mrs. Norris, 'that Dr. Grant hardly knows what the natural taste of our apricot is: he is scarcely ever indulged with one, for it is so valuable a fruit; with a little assistance, and ours is such a remarkably large, fair sort, that what with early tarts and preserves, my cook contrives to get them all.'

Mrs. Norris, who had begun to redden, was appeased; and, for a little while, other subjects took place of the improvements of Sotherton. Dr. Grant and Mrs. Norris were seldom good friends; their acquaintance had begun in dilapidations, and their habits were totally dissimilar.

After a short interruption Mr. Rushworth began again. 'Smith's place is the admiration of all the country; and it was a mere nothing before Repton took it in hand. I think I shall have Repton.'

'Mr. Rushworth,' said Lady Bertram, 'if I were you, I would have a very pretty shrubbery. One likes to get out into a shrubbery in fine weather.'

Mr. Rushworth was eager to assure her ladyship of his acquiescence, and tried to make out something complimentary; but, between his submission

to *her* taste, and his having always intended the same himself, with the superadded objects of professing attention to the comfort of ladies in general, and of insinuating that there was one only whom he was anxious to please, he grew puzzled, and Edmund was glad to put an end to his speech by a proposal of wine. Mr. Rushworth, however, though not usually a great talker, had still more to say on the subject next his heart. 'Smith has not much above a hundred acres altogether in his grounds, which is little enough, and makes it more surprising that the place can have been so improved. Now, at Sotherton we have a good seven hundred, without reckoning the water meadows; so that I think, if so much could be done at

Compton, we need not despair. There have been two or three fine old trees cut down, that grew too near the house, and it opens the prospect amazingly, which makes me think that Repton, or anybody of that sort, would certainly have the avenue at Sotherton down: the avenue that leads from the west front to the top of the hill, you know,' turning to Miss Bertram particularly as he spoke. But Miss Bertram thought it most becoming to reply –

'The avenue! Oh! I do not recollect it. I really know very little of Sotherton.'

Fanny, who was sitting on the other side of Edmund, exactly opposite Miss Crawford, and who had been attentively listening, now looked at him, and said in a low voice –

'Cut down an avenue! What a pity! Does it not make you think of Cowper? "Ye fallen avenues, once more I mourn your fate unmerited." '

He smiled as he answered, 'I am afraid the avenue stands a bad chance, Fanny.'

'I should like to see Sotherton before it is cut down, to see the place as it is now, in its old state; but I do not suppose I shall.'

'Have you never been there? No, you never can; and, unluckily, it is out of distance for a ride. I wish we could contrive it.'

'Oh! it does not signify. Whenever I do see it, you will tell me how it has been altered.'

'I collect,' said Miss Crawford, 'that Sotherton is an old place, and a place of some grandeur. In any particular style of building?'

'The house was built in Elizabeth's time, and is a large, regular, brick building; heavy, but respectable looking, and has many good rooms. It is ill placed. It stands in one of the lowest spots of the park; in that respect, unfavourable for improvement. But the woods are fine, and there is a stream, which, I dare say, might be made a good deal of. Mr. Rushworth is quite right, I think, in meaning to give it a modern dress, and I have no doubt that it will be all done extremely well.'

Miss Crawford listened with submission, and said to herself, 'He is a well-bred man; he makes the best of it.'

'I do not wish to influence Mr. Rushworth,' he continued; 'but, had I a place to new fashion, I should not put myself into the hands of an improver. I would rather have an inferior degree of beauty, of my own choice, and acquired progressively. I would rather abide by my own blunders than by his.'

'*You* would know what you were about, of course; but that would not suit *me*. I have no eye or ingenuity for such matters, but as they are before me; and had I a place of my own in the country, I should be most thankful to any Mr. Repton who would undertake it, and give me as much beauty as he could for my money; and I should never look at it till it was complete.'

'It would be delightful to *me* to see the progress of it all,' said Fanny.

Thomas Love Peacock
Headlong Hall, 1816

'I perceive,' said Mr Milestone, after they had walked a few paces, 'these grounds have never been touched by the finger of taste.'

'The place is quite a wilderness,' said Squire Headlong: 'for, during the latter part of my father's life, while I was *finishing my education*, he troubled himself about nothing but the cellar, and suffered everything else to go to rack and ruin. A mere wilderness, as you see, even now in December; but in summer a complete nursery of briers, a forest of thistles, a plantation of nettles, without any livestock but goats, that have eaten up all the bark of the trees. Here you see is the pedestal of a statue, with only half a leg and four toes remaining: there were many here once. When I was a boy, I used to sit every day on the shoulders of Hercules: what became of *him* I have never been able to ascertain. Neptune has been lying these seven years in the dust-hole; Atlas had his head knocked off to fit him for propping a shed; and only the day before yesterday we fished Bacchus out of the horse-pond.'

'My dear sir,' said Mr Milestone, 'accord me your permission to wave the wand of enchantment over your grounds. The rocks shall be blown up, the trees shall be cut down, the wilderness and all its goats shall vanish like mist. Pagodas and Chinese bridges, gravel walks and shrubberies, bowling-greens, canals, and clumps of larch, shall rise upon its ruins. One age, sir, has brought to light the treasures of ancient learning; a second has penetrated into the depths of metaphysics; a third has brought to perfection the science of astronomy; but it was reserved for the exclusive genius of the present times, to invent the noble art of picturesque gardening, which has given, as it were, a new tint to the complexion of nature, and a new outline to the physiognomy of the universe!'

'Give me leave,' said Sir Patrick O'Prism, 'to take an exception to that same. Your system of levelling, and trimming, and clipping, and docking, and clumping, and polishing, and cropping, and shaving, destroys all the beautiful intricacies of natural luxuriance, and all the graduated harmonies of light and shade, melting into one another, as you see them on that rock over yonder. I never saw one of your improved places, as you call them, and which are nothing but big bowling-greens, like sheets of green paper, with a parcel of round clumps scattered over them, like so many spots of ink, flicked at random out of a pen, and a solitary animal here and there looking as if it were lost, that I did not think it was for all the world like Hounslow Heath, thinly sprinkled over with bushes and highwaymen.'

'Sir,' said Mr Milestone, 'you will have the goodness to make a distinction between the picturesque and the beautiful.'

'Will I?' said Sir Patrick, 'och! but I won't. For what is beautiful? That which pleases the eye. And what pleases the eye? Tints variously broken and blended. Now, tints variously broken and blended constitute the picturesque.'

'Allow me,' said Mr Gall. 'I distinguish the picturesque and the beautiful, and I add to them, in the laying out of grounds, a third and distinct character, which I call *unexpectedness.*'

'Pray, sir,' said Mr Milestone, 'by what name do you distinguish this character, when a person walks round the grounds for the second time?'

Mr Gall bit his lips, and inwardly vowed to revenge himself on Milestone, by cutting up his next publication.

A long controversy now ensued concerning the picturesque and the beautiful, highly edifying to Squire Headlong.

Mr Milestone had produced his portfolio for the edification and amusement of Miss Tenorina, Miss Graziosa, and Squire Headlong, to whom he was pointing out the various beauties of his plan for Lord Littlebrain's park.

MR MILESTONE   This, you perceive, is the natural state of one part of the grounds. Here is a wood, never yet touched by the finger of taste; thick, intricate, and gloomy. Here is a little stream, dashing from stone to stone, and overshadowed with these untrimmed boughs.

MISS TENORINA   The sweet romantic spot! How beautifully the birds must sing there on a summer evening!

MISS GRAZIOSA   Dear sister! how can you endure the horrid thicket?

MR MILESTONE   You are right, Miss Graziosa: your taste is correct – perfectly *en règle*. Now, here is the same place corrected – trimmed – polished – decorated – adorned. Here sweeps a plantation, in that beautiful regular curve: there winds a gravel walk: here are parts of the old wood, left in these majestic circular clumps, disposed at equal distances with wonderful symmetry: there are some single shrubs scattered in elegant profusion: here a Portugal laurel, there a juniper; here a lauristinus, there a spruce fir; here a larch, there a lilac; here a rhododendron, there an arbutus. The stream, you see, become a canal: the banks are perfectly smooth and green; sloping to the water's edge: and there is Lord Littlebrain, rowing in an elegant boat.

SQUIRE HEADLONG Magical, faith!

MR MILESTONE   Here is another part of the grounds in its natural state. Here is a large rock, with the mountain-ash rooted in its fissures, overgrown, as you see, with ivy and moss;

and from this part of it bursts a little fountain, that runs bubbling down its rugged sides.

MISS TENORINA   O how beautiful! How I should love the melody of that miniature cascade.

MR MILESTONE   Beautiful, Miss Tenorina! Hideous. Base, common, and popular. Such a thing as you may see anywhere, in wild and mountainous districts. Now, observe the metamorphosis. Here is the same rock, cut into the shape of a giant. In one hand he holds a horn, through which that little fountain is thrown to a prodigious elevation. In the other is a ponderous stone, so exactly balanced as to be apparently ready to fall on the head of any person who may happen to be beneath: and there is Lord Littlebrain walking under it.

SQUIRE HEADLONG Miraculous, by Mahomet!

MR MILESTONE   This is the summit of a hill, covered, as you perceive, with wood, and with those mossy stones scattered at random under the trees.

MISS TENORINA   What a delightful spot to read in, on a summer's day! The air must be so pure, and the wind must sound so divinely in the tops of those old pines!

MR MILESTONE   Bad taste, Miss Tenorina. Bad taste, I assure you. Here is the spot improved. The trees are cut down: the stones are cleared away: this is an octagonal pavilion, exactly on the centre of the summit: and there you see Lord

Littlebrain, on the top of the pavilion, enjoying the prospect with a telescope.

SQUIRE HEADLONG Glorious, egad!

MR MILESTONE Here is a rugged mountainous road, leading through impervious shades: the ass and the four goats characterise a wild uncultured scene. Here, as you perceive, it is totally changed into a beautiful gravel-road, gracefully curving through a belt of limes: and there is Lord Littlebrain driving four-in-hand.

SQUIRE HEADLONG Egregious, by Jupiter!

MR MILESTONE Here is Littlebrain Castle, a Gothic, moss-grown structure, half-bosomed in trees. Near the casement of that turret is an owl peeping from the ivy.

SQUIRE HEADLONG And devilish wise he looks.

MR MILESTONE Here is the new house, without a tree near it, standing in the midst of an undulating lawn: a white, polished, angular building, reflected to a nicety in this waveless lake: and there you see Lord Littlebrain looking out of the window.

SQUIRE HEADLONG And devilish wise he looks too. You shall cut me a giant before you go.

MR MILESTONE Good. I'll order down my little corps of pioneers.

Joseph Addison
The Spectator No. 477, 1712

Sir,

Having lately read your Essay on the Pleasures of the Imagination, I was so taken with your Thoughts upon some of our *English* Gardens, that I cannot forbear troubling you with a Letter upon that Subject. I am one, you must know, who am looked upon as an Humorist in Gardening. I have several Acres about my House, which I call my Garden, and which a skilful Gardener would not know what to call. It is a Confusion of Kitchin and Parterre, Orchard and Flower-Garden, which lie so mixt and interwoven with one another, that if a Foreigner who had seen nothing of our Country should be convey'd into my Garden at his first landing, he would look upon it as a natural Wilderness, and one of the uncultivated Parts of our Country. My Flowers grow up in several Parts of the Garden in the greatest Luxuriancy and Profusion. I am so far from being fond of any particular one, by reason of its Rarity, that if I meet with any one in a Field which pleases me, I give it a place in my Garden. By this means, when a Stranger walks with me, he is surprized to see several large Spots of Ground cover'd with ten thousand different Colours, and has often singled out Flowers that he might have met with under a common Hedge, in a Field, or in a Meadow, as some of the greatest Beauties of the Place. The only Method I observe in this Particular, is to range in the same Quarter the Products of the same Season, that they may make their Appearance together, and compose a Picture of the greatest Variety. There is the same Irregularity in my Plantations, which run into as great a Wildness as their Natures will permit. I take in none that do not naturally rejoice in the Soil, and am pleased when I am walking in a Labyrinth of my own raising, not to know whether the next Tree I shall meet with is an Apple or an Oak, an Elm or a Pear-Tree. My Kitchin has likewise its particular Quarters assigned it; for besides the wholesome Luxury which that Place abounds with, I have always thought a Kitchin-Garden a more pleasant Sight than the finest Orangery, or artificial Greenhouse. I love to see everything in its Perfection, and am more pleased to survey my Rows of Coleworts and Cabbages, with a thousand nameless Pot-herbs, springing up in their full Fragrancy and Verdure, than to see the tender Plants of Foreign Countries kept alive by artificial Heats, or withering in an Air and Soil that are not adapted to them. I must not omit, that there is a Fountain rising in the upper part of my Garden, which forms a little wandring Rill, and administers to the Pleasure as well as the Plenty of the Place. I have so conducted it, that it visits most of my Plantations; and have taken particular Care to let it run in the same manner as it would do in an open Field, so that it generally passes through Banks of Violets and Primroses, Plats of Willow, or other Plants, that seem to be of its own producing. There is another Circumstance in which I am very particular, or, as my Neighbours call me, very whimsical: As my Garden invites into it all the Birds of the Country, by offering them the Conveniency of Springs and Shades, Solitude and Shelter, I do not suffer any one to destroy their Nests in the Spring, or drive them from their usual Haunts in Fruit-time. I value my Garden more for being full of Blackbirds than Cherries, and very frankly give them Fruit for their Songs. By this means I have always the Musick of the Season in its Perfection, and am highly delighted to see the Jay or the Thrush hopping about my Walks, and shooting before my Eye across the several little Glades and Alleys that I pass thro'. I think there are as many kinds of Gardening as of Poetry: Your Makers of Parterres and Flower-Gardens, are Epigrammatists and Sonneteers in this Art; Contrivers of Bowers and Grotto's, Treillages and Cascades, are Romance Writers. *Wise* and *London* are our heroick Poets; and if, as a Critick, I may single out any Passage of their Works to commend, I shall take notice of that Part in the upper Garden at *Kensington*, which was at first nothing but a Gravel-Pit. It must have been a fine Genius for Gardening, that could have thought of forming such an unsightly Hollow into so beautiful an Area, and to have hit the Eye with so uncommon and agreeable a Scene as that which it is now wrought into. To give this particular Spot of Ground the greater Effect, they have made a very pleasing Contrast; for as on one side of the Walk you see this hollow Basin, with its several little Plantations lying so conveniently under the Eye of the Beholder; on the other side of it there appears a seeming Mount, made up of Trees rising one higher than another in proportion as they approach the Center. A Spectator, who has not heard this Account of it, would think this Circular Mount was not only a real one, but that it had been actually scooped out of that hollow Space which I have before mention'd. I never yet met with any one who had walked in this Garden, who was not struck with that Part of it which I have here mention'd. As for my self, you will find, by the Account which I have already given you, that my Compositions in Gardening are altogether after the *Pindarick* Manner, and run into the beautiful Wildness of Nature, without affecting the nicer Elegancies of Art. What I am now going to mention, will, perhaps, deserve your Attention more than any thing I have yet said. I find that in the Discourse which I spoke of at the Beginning of my Letter, you are against filling an *English* Garden with Ever-Greens; and indeed I am so far of your Opinion, that I can by no means think the Verdure of an Ever-Green comparable to that which shoots out annually, and clothes our Trees in the Summer-Season. But I have often wonder'd that those who are like my self, and love to live in Gardens, have never thought of contriving a *Winter-Garden*, which would consist of such Trees only as never cast their Leaves. We have very often little Snatches of

Sunshine and fair Weather in the most uncomfortable Parts of the Year; and have frequently several Days in *November* and *January* that are as agreeable as any in the finest Months. At such times, therefore, I think there could not be a greater Pleasure, than to walk in such a *Winter-Garden* as I have proposed. In the Summer-Season the whole Country blooms, and is a kind of Garden, for which reason we are not so sensible of those Beauties that at this time may be every where met with; but when Nature is in her Desolation, and presents us with nothing but bleak and barren Prospects, there is something unspeakably chearful in a Spot of Ground which is covered with Trees that smile amidst all the Rigours of Winter, and give us a View of the most gay Season in the midst of that which is the most dead and melancholy. I have so far indulged my self in this Thought, that I have set apart a whole Acre of Ground for the executing of it. The Walls are covered with Ivy instead of Vines. The Laurel, the Hornbeam, and the Holly, with many other Trees and Plants of the same nature, grow so thick in it, that you cannot imagine a more lively Scene. The glowing Redness of the Berries, with which they are hung at this time, vies with the Verdure of their Leaves, and are apt to inspire the Heart of the Beholder with that vernal Delight which you have somewhere taken notice of in your former papers. It is very pleasant, at the same time, to see the several kinds of Birds retiring into this little Green Spot, and enjoying themselves among the Branches and Foliage, when my great Garden, which I have before mention'd to you, does not afford a single Leaf for their Shelter.

You must know, Sir, that I look upon the Pleasure which we take in a Garden, as one of the most innocent Delights in Human Life. A Garden was the Habitation of our first Parents before the Fall. It is naturally apt to fill the Mind with Calmness and Tranquillity, and to lay all its turbulent Passions at rest. It gives us a great insight into the Contrivance and Wisdom of Providence, and suggests innumerable Subjects for Meditation. I cannot but think the very Complacency and Satisfaction which a Man takes in these Works of Nature, to be a laudable, if not a virtuous Habit of Mind. For all which Reasons I hope you will pardon the Length of my present Letter.

Oliver Goldsmith
The Citizen of the World, 1762

The English have not yet brought the art of gardening to the same perfection with the Chinese, but have lately begun to imitate them; Nature is now followed with greater assiduity than formerly; the trees are suffered to shoot out into the utmost luxuriance; the streams no longer forced from their native beds, are permitted to wind along the vallies: spontaneous flowers take the place of the finished parterre, and the enamelled meadow of the shaven green.

Yet still the English are far behind us in this charming art: their designers have not yet attained a power of uniting instruction with beauty. An European will scarcely conceive my meaning, when I say, that there is scarce a garden in China which does not contain some fine moral, couch'd under the general design, where one is not taught wisdom as he walks, and feels the force of some noble truth or delicate precept resulting from the disposition of the groves, streams or grotto's.

Permit me to illustrate what I mean by a description of my gardens at Quamsi. My heart still hovers round those scenes of former happiness with pleasure; and I find satisfaction in enjoying them at this distance, though but in imagination.

You descended from the house between two groves of trees, planted in such a manner that they were impenetrable to the eye; while on each hand the way was adorned with all that was beautiful in porcelaine, statuary and painting.

This passage from the house opened into an area surrounded with rocks, flowers, trees and shrubs, but all so disposed as if each was the spontaneous production of nature. As you proceeded forward on this lawn, to your right and left hand were two gates, opposite each other, of very different architecture and design; and before you lay a temple built rather with minute elegance than ostentation.

The right-hand gate was planned with the utmost simplicity or rather rudeness; ivy clasp'd round the pillars, the baleful cyprus hung over it; time seemed to have destroyed all the smoothness and regularity of the stone: two champions with lifted clubs appeared in the act of guarding its access; dragons and serpents were seen in the most hideous attitudes, to deter the spectator from approaching; and the perspective view that lay behind seemed dark and gloomy to the last degree; the stranger was tempted to enter only from the motto: PERVIA VIRTUTI.

The opposite gate was formed in a very different manner; the architecture was light, elegant and inviting; flowers hung in wreaths round the pillars; all was finished in the most exact and masterly manner; the very stone of which it was built still preserved its polish; nymphs wrought by the hand of a master, in the most alluring attitudes, beckoned the stranger to approach, while all that lay behind as far as the eye could reach, seemed gay, luxuriant, and capable of affording endless pleasure. The motto itself contributed to invite him; for over the gate was written these words, FACILIS DESCENSUS.

William Shenstone
'Unconnected Thoughts on Gardening'
The Works in Verse and Prose, 1764

Art should never be allowed to set a foot in the province of nature, otherwise than clandestinely and by night. Whenever she is allowed to appear here, and men begin to compromise the difference – night, gothicism, confusion and absolute chaos, are come again.

The works of a person that builds, begin immediately to decay; while those of him who plants begin directly to improve. In this, planting promises a more lasting pleasure, than building; which, were it to remain in equal perfection, would at best begin to moulder and want repair in imagination. Now trees have a circumstance that suits our taste, and that is annual variety. It is inconvenient indeed, if they cause our love of life to take root and flourish with them; whereas the very sameness of our structures will, without the help of dilapidation, serve to wean us from our attachement to them.

It is a custom in some countries to condemn the characters of those (after death) that have neither planted a tree, nor begot a child.

Alexander Pope
The Guardian 173, 1713

How contrary to this Simplicity is the modern Practice of Gardening; we seem to make it our Study to recede from Nature, not only in the various Tonsure of Greens into the most regular and formal Shapes, but even in monstrous Attempts beyond the reach of the Art it self: We run into Sculpture, and are yet better pleas'd to have our Trees in the most awkward Figures of Men and Animals, than in the most regular of their own. . . .

I believe it is no wrong Observation that Persons of Genius, and those who are most capable of Art, are always most fond of Nature, as such are chiefly sensible, that all Art consists in the Imitation and Study of Nature. On the contrary, People of the common Level of Understanding are principally delighted with the little Niceties and Fantastical Operations of Art, and constantly think that *finest* which is least Natural. A Citizen is no sooner Proprietor of a couple of Yews, but he entertains Thoughts of erecting them into Giants, like those of *Guild-hall*. I know an eminent Cook, who beautified his Country Seat with a Coronation Dinner in Greens, where you see the Champion flourishing on Horseback at one end of the Table, and the Queen in perpetual Youth at the other.

For the benefit of all my loving Countrymen of this curious Taste, I shall here publish a Catalogue of Greens to be disposed of by an eminent Town-Gardiner, who has lately applied to me upon this Head. He represents, that for the Advancement of a politer sort of Ornament in the Villa's and

Gardens adjacent to this great City, and in order to distinguish those Places from the meer barbarous Countries of gross Nature, the World stands much in need of a Virtuoso Gardiner who has a Turn to Sculpture, and is thereby capable of improving upon the Ancients of his Profession in the Imagery of Evergreens. My Correspondent is arrived to such Perfection, that he cuts Family Pieces of Men, Women or Children. Any Ladies that please may have their own Effigies in Myrtle, or their Husbands in Hornbeam. He is a Puritan Wag, and never fails, when he shows his Garden, to repeat that Passage in the Psalms, *Thy Wife shall be as the fruitful Vine, and thy Children as Olive Branches round thy Table*. I shall proceed to his Catalogue, as he sent it for my Recommendation.

Adam and *Eve* in yew; *Adam* a little shatter'd by the fall of the Tree of Knowledge in the great Storm; *Eve* and the Serpent very flourishing.

The Tower of *Babel*, not yet finished.

St. *George* in Box; his Arm scarce long enough, but will be in a Condition to stick the Dragon by next *April*.

A *green Dragon* of the same, with a Tail of Ground Ivy for the present.

N.B. *These two not to be Sold separately*.

Edward the Black Prince in Cypress.

A *Laurustine* Bear in Blossom, with a Juniper Hunter in Berries.

A Pair of Giants, *stunted*, to be sold cheap.

A Queen *Elizabeth* in Phylyræa, a little inclining to the Green Sickness, but of full growth.

Another Queen *Elizabeth* in Myrtle, which was very forward, but Miscarried by being too near a Savine.

An old Maid of Honour in Wormwood.

A topping *Ben Johnson* in Lawrel.

Divers eminent Modern Poets in Bays, somewhat blighted, to be disposed of a Pennyworth.

A Quick-set Hog shot up into a Porcupine, by its being forgot a Week in rainy Weather.

A Lavender Pigg with Sage growing in his Belly.

Noah's Ark in Holly, standing on the Mount; the Ribs a little damaged for want of Water.

A Pair of *Maidenheads* in Firr, in great forwardness.

William Wordsworth
Letter to Lady Beaumont, *3 February*, 1807

My dear Lady Beaumont,

Lord Redesdale's letter contains several things that will be of use to us; I must however make two or three remarks upon it. Our garden is to be a winter garden, a place of comfort and pleasure from the fall of the leaf to its return – nearly half of the year. Great part of this time you now perhaps pass in London, but if you live that probably will not always be so. Infirmities come on with age, that render tranquillity every year more welcome and more necessary. Lord Redesdale seems to have overlooked this, as far as the greatest part of his letter applies to a summer garden. His plan of avoiding expense in digging, weeding, and mowing – particularly the last – may be carried too far; a wilderness of shrubs is a delightful thing as part of a garden, but only as a part. You must have open space of lawn, or you lose all the beauty of outline in the different tufts or islands of shrubs, and even in many instances in their individual forms. This lawn cannot be had without mowing. Digging and weeding ought to be avoided as much as possible; and his method is a good one. With his Lordship, I should wish my strength to lie in perennial plants and flowers; but a small quantity of annuals, such as flower very late, may with little trouble and great advantage be interspersed among the others. His objection to an over-arched walk of evergreens, except for summer, at first appears well founded; but there is an oversight in it. In summer you may have a shade

of deciduous trees or plants; but what are you to do in April or March, and sometimes even in February, when the heat and glare of the sun are often oppressive, notwithstanding the general cloudiness of our climate? For my own part, I can say with truth that in the month of April I have passed many an hour under the shade of a green holly, glad to find it in my walk, and unwilling to quit it because I had not courage to face the sun. Our winter garden is four parts out of five planned for the sun. If the alley or bower, the only parts exclusively designed for shade, should appear too damp or gloomy, you pass them by; but I am sure this will not always be the case; and even in those times when it is so, will not a peep into that gloom make you enjoy the sunshine the more? But the alley I designed for March and April, when there is often a heat in the sun, and a conflict of sun and wind, which is both unpleasant and dangerous, and from which neither walls nor bare leafless trees can protect you. . . . His Lordship's practical rules about making walks, propagating plants, etc., seem all to be excellent; and I much like his plan of a covered walk of vines – but not for our own winter garden.

Sir Walter Scott
'On Landscape Gardening'
Quarterly Review, 1828

We ourselves retain an early and pleasing recollection of the seclusion of such a scene. A small cottage, adjacent to a beautiful village, the habitation of an ancient maiden lady, was for some time our abode. It was situated in a garden of seven or eight acres, planted about the beginning of the eighteenth century by one of the Millars, related to the author of the *Gardener's Dictionary*, or, for aught we know, by himself. It was full of long straight walks betwixt hedges of yew and horn-beam, which rose tall and close on every side. There were thickets of flowering shrubs, a bower, and an arbour, to which access was obtained through a little maze of contorted walks, calling itself a labyrinth. In the centre of the bower was a splendid platanus, or Oriental plane – a huge hill of leaves – one of the noblest specimens of that regularly beautiful tree which we remember to have seen. In different parts of the garden were fine ornamental trees which had attained great size, and the orchard was filled with fruit-trees of the best description. There were seats and trellis-walks, and a banqueting-house. Even in our time, this little scene, intended to present a formal exhibition of vegetable beauty, was going fast to decay. The parterres of flowers were no longer watched by the quiet and simple *friends* under whose auspices they had been planted, and much of the ornament of the domain had been neglected or destroyed to increase its productive value. We visited it lately,

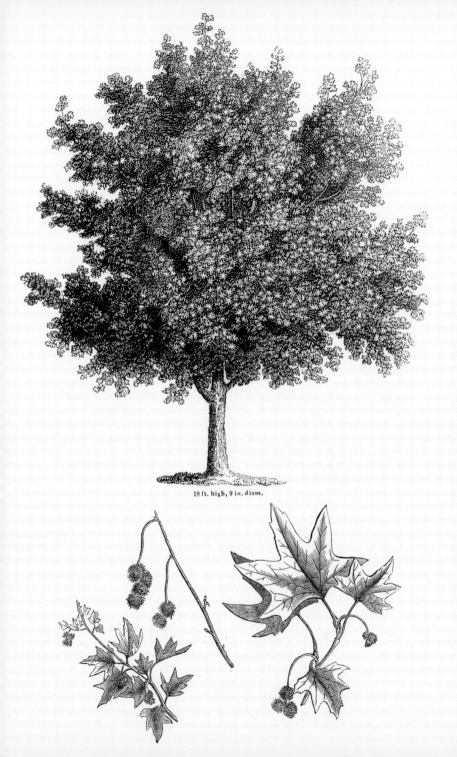

18 ft. high, 9 in. diam.

after an absence of many years. Its air of retreat, the seclusion which its alleys afforded, was entirely gone; the huge platanus had died, like most of its kind, in the beginning of this century; the hedges were cut down, the trees stubbed up, and the whole character of the place so much destroyed, that we were glad when we could leave it. This was the progress of innovation, perhaps of improvement: yet, for the sake of that one garden, as a place of impressive and solemn retreat, we are inclined to enter a protest against the hasty and ill-considered destruction of things which, once destroyed, cannot be restored. . . .

Those who choose to prosecute this subject farther, will find in Sir U. Price's book his regret for the destruction of a garden on the old system, described in a tone of exquisite feeling, which leads that distinguished author to declare in favour of many parts of the old school of gardening, and to argue for the preservation of the few remains of ancient magnificence that still exist, by awakening the owner to a sense of their beauties.

It were indeed high time that some one should interfere. The garden, artificial in its structure, its shelter, its climate, and its soil, which every consideration of taste, beauty, and convenience recommended to be kept near to the mansion, and maintained, as its appendage, in the highest state of ornamental decoration which could be used with reference to the character of the house itself, has, by a strange and sweeping sentence of exile, been condemned to wear the coarsest and most humbling form. Reduced to a clumsy oblong, enclosed within four rough-built walls, and sequestered in some distant corner where it may be best concealed from the eye to which it has been rendered a nuisance, the modern garden resembles nothing so much as a convict in his gaol apparel, banished, by his very appearance, from all decent society. If the peculiarity of the proprietor's taste inclines him to the worship of Flora or Pomona, he must attend their rites in distance and secrecy, as if he were practising some abhorred mysteries, instead of rendering an homage which is so peculiarly united with that of the household gods.

Uvedale Price
'On the Picturesque', 1794

If we turn from animal to vegetable nature, many of the most beautiful flowers have a high degree of symmetry; so much so, that their colours appear to be laid on after a regular and finished design: but beauty is so much the prevailing character of flowers, that no one seeks for any thing picturesque among them. In trees, on the other hand, every thing appears so loose and irregular, that symmetry seems out of the question; yet still the same analogy subsists. Cowley has very accurately enumerated the chief qualities of beauty, in his description of what he considers as one of the most beautiful of trees – the lime. He has not forgot symmetry in the catalogue of its charms, though it is probable that few readers will agree with him in admiring the degree or the style of it, which is displayed in the lime: but exact symmetry in all things was then extravagantly in fashion, as it is now – perhaps too violently – in disgrace. . . .

  A *beautiful tree*, considered in point of form only, must have a certain correspondence of parts, and a comparative regularity of proportion; whereas inequality and irregularity alone will give to a tree a picturesque appearance, more especially if the effects of age as well as of accident are conspicuous: when, for instance, some of the limbs are shattered, and the broken stump remains in the void space; when others, half twisted round by winds, hand downwards; while others again shoot in an opposite direction, and perhaps some large bough projects sideways from below the

Tiliaceae

Tilia europaea

Common Lime

(long-lived tree)

stag-headed top, and then suddenly turns upwards, and rises above it. The general proportions of such trees, whether tall or short, thick or slender, is not material to their character as *picturesque* objects; but where beauty, elegance, and gracefulness are concerned, a short thick proportion will not give an idea of those qualities. There certainly are a great variety of pleasing forms and proportions in trees, and different men have different predilections, just as they have with respect to their own species; but I never knew any person, who, if he observed at all, was not struck with the gracefulness and elegance of a tree, whose proportion was rather tall, whose stem had an easy sweep, but which returned again in such a manner, that the whole appeared completely poised and balanced, and whose boughs were in some degree pendent, but towards their extremities made a gentle curve upwards: if to such a form you add fresh foliage and bark, you have every quality assigned to beauty.

Gustave Flaubert
Bouvard et Pécuchet, 1881

It was first necessary to have good hotbeds. Pécuchet had them built of brick. He painted the frames himself, and for fear of too much sun, whitewashed all the glass cloches.

He took the precaution of choosing leafy tops for his cuttings. Then he applied himself to layering. He attempted all sorts of grafts, grafts *en flute*, crown grafts, bud grafts, herbaceous grafts, English grafts. With what care he adjusted the stock and the scion! How he tightened the bindings! With what masses of wax he covered the joints!

Twice a day he took his watering can and swung it above the plants as though it were a censer. As they turned green under the fine sprinkling, he felt as though his own thirst was being slaked and that he too was coming back to life. In an access of excitement, he tore the rose off the watering can and poured a copious stream straight out of the spout.

Next to the arbour near the plaster lady rose a sort of shed made of logs. Pécuchet kept his tools there, and there passed delightful hours shelling seeds, writing labels, and putting his little pots in order. He would rest sitting on a box in front of the door, contemplating improvements in his garden.

At the foot of the steps he had placed two pots of geraniums; between the cypresses and the cordons he planted sunflowers; and since the flower beds were covered with buttercups and all the paths with fresh sand, the garden was dazzlingly yellow.

But the hotbeds swarmed with grubs; despite the covering of dead leaves, under the painted frames and the whitewashed glass the vegetation was spindly. The cuttings did not take; the grafts came apart; the runners dried up, the tree roots turned white with rot; the seed-beds were a wasteland. The wind amused itself by toppling the bean frames. Too much fertilizer spoiled the strawberries, a shortage of nourishment did for the tomatoes.

He missed out on broccoli, aubergines, turnips – and on watercress, which he had intended to raise in a trough. In the wake of a frost, all the artichokes died.

The cabbages consoled him. One, above all, gave him great hope. It spread out, grew tall, and at length became prodigious and absolutely inedible. No matter! Pécuchet was content to possess a monster.

He then decided to try what seemed to him the height of the art – raising melons.

He sowed the seeds of many varieties in trays of potting soil, which he sank in his hotbed. Then he prepared another hotbed; when it had started to give out heat he planted the strongest seedlings, covering them with cloches. Following the instructions of the gardening manual to the letter, he snipped off the excess blossoms; once the plants had set fruit, he chose one fruit on each stem and removed the others; and when the fruits were the size of a nut, he slid a small board under each to prevent their rotting from contact with the manure. He warmed them, aired them, wiped the mist from the cloches with his handkerchief – and when clouds approached rushed out with straw mats to shelter them. At night, he did not sleep. On many occasions he arose;

and with his feet bare in his boots, wearing a nightshirt and shivering, he crossed the garden to lay his eiderdown over the frames.

The cantaloupes ripened.

The first brought a grimace to Bouvard's face. The second was no better, nor was the third. For each Pécuchet found a new excuse, until the last, which he pitched out of the window declaring that he couldn't understand it.

The fact was that he had planted different varieties next to one another, the sweet next to the bitter, *le gros Portugal* next to *le grand Mogol* – with the proximity of the tomato patch completing the anarchy. The result was an abominable crossbreed that tasted like a pumpkin.

Pécuchet turned to flowers. He wrote to Dumouchel for shrubs and seeds, bought a supply of compost and set resolutely to work.

But he planted passion-flowers in the shade, pansies in the sun, covered the hyacinths with manure, watered the lilies after they had flowered, destroyed the rhododendrons with heavy pruning, stimulated the fuchsias with glue, and roasted a pomegranate to death by exposing it to the fire in the kitchen.

At the approach of cold weather, he sheltered the rosebushes with domes of paper waterproofed with candlegrease; they looked like sugar loaves perched on sticks. Huge stakes held up the dahlias – between their straight ranks could be seen the twisted branches of a sophora japonica that clung to life without dying but without growing, either . . .

All his experiments failed. Each time he was greatly surprised.

III

INTIMATE ENGAGEMENT

The private garden – the garden with flowers and shrubs and a scale that made it feasible for ordinary people living in ordinary houses – came to the fore in the nineteenth century, largely due to the efforts of journalists like John Claudius Loudon. Gardening was less a matter of instructing staff and more of personal engagement with spade and hoe. There was still the literary approach of such eloquent horticultural philosophers as Canon Henry Ellacombe and later Sir George Sitwell, but the authentic tone of the time may better be found in down-to-earth writers like William Cobbett, or certain Americans: newspaperman Charles Dudley Warner and the inimitable Henry David Thoreau. And in case all seemed too settled, there was the magisterial William Robinson loudly arguing that gardens should be 'wild' and Reginald Blomfield that they should be 'formal'. Neither won – or lost.

Charles Dudley Warner
My Summer in a Garden, 1871

Next to deciding when to start your garden, the most important matter is, what to put in it. It is difficult to decide what to order for dinner on a given day: how much more oppressive is it to order in a lump an endless vista of dinners, so to speak! For, unless your garden is a boundless prairie (and mine seems to me to be that when I hoe it on hot days), you must make a selection, from the great variety of vegetables, of those you will raise in it; and you feel rather bound to supply your own table from your own garden, and to eat only as you have sown.

I hold that no man has a right (whatever his sex, of course) to have a garden to his own selfish uses. He ought not to please himself, but every man to please his neighbor. I tried to have a garden that would give general moral satisfaction. It seemed to me that nobody could object to potatoes (a most useful vegetable); and I began to plant them freely. But there was a chorus of protest against them. 'You don't want to take up your ground with potatoes,' the neighbors said; 'you can buy potatoes' (the very thing I wanted to avoid doing is buying things). 'What you want is the perishable things that you cannot get fresh in the market.' 'But what kind of perishable things?' A horticulturist of eminence wanted me to sow lines of strawberries and raspberries right over where I had put my potatoes in drills. I had about five hundred strawberry-plants in another part of my garden; but this fruit-fanatic wanted me to turn my whole patch into vines and runners. I suppose I could raise strawberries enough for all my neighbors; and perhaps I ought to do it. I had a little space prepared for melons – muskmelons – which I showed to an experienced friend.

'You are not going to waste your ground on muskmelons?' he asked. 'They rarely ripen in this climate thoroughly, before frost.' He had tried for years without luck. I resolved to not go into such a foolish experiment. But, the next day, another neighbor happened in. 'Ah! I see you are going to have melons. My family would rather give up anything else in the garden than muskmelons, of the nutmeg variety. They are the most grateful things we have on the table.' So there it was. There was no compromise: it was melons, or no melons, and somebody offended in any case. I half resolved to plant them a little late, so that they would, and they wouldn't. But I had the same difficulty about string-beans (which I detest), and squash (which I tolerate), and parsnips, and the whole round of green things.

I have pretty much come to the conclusion that you have got to put your foot down in gardening. If I had actually taken counsel of my friends, I should not have had a thing growing in the garden to-day but weeds. And besides, while you are waiting, Nature does not wait. Her mind is made up. She knows just what she will raise; and she has an infinite variety of early and late. The most humiliating thing to me about a garden is the lesson it teaches of the inferiority of man. Nature is prompt, decided, inexhaustible. She thrusts up her plants with a vigor and freedom that I admire; and the more worthless the plant, the more rapid and splendid its growth. She is at it early and late, and all night; never tiring, nor showing the least sign of exhaustion.

'Eternal gardening is the price of liberty,' is a motto that I should put over the gateway of my garden, if I had a gate. And yet it is not wholly true; for there is no liberty in gardening. The man who undertakes a garden is relentlessly pursued. He felicitates himself that, when he gets it once planted, he will have a season of rest and of enjoyment in the sprouting and growing of his seeds. It is a green anticipation. He has planted a seed that will keep him awake nights; drive rest from his bones, and sleep from his pillow. Hardly is the garden planted, when he must begin to hoe it. The weeds have sprung up all over it in a night. They shine and wave in redundant life. The docks have almost gone to seed; and their roots go deeper than conscience. Talk about the London Docks! – the roots of these are like the sources of the Aryan race. And the weeds are not all. I awake in the morning (and a thriving garden will wake a person up two hours before he ought to be out of bed) and think of the tomato-plants – the leaves like fine lace-work, owing to black bugs that skip around, and can't be caught. Somebody ought to get up before the dew is off (why don't the dew stay on till after a reasonable breakfast?) and sprinkle soot on the leaves. I wonder if it is I. Soot is so much blacker than the bugs, that they are disgusted, and go away. You can't get up too early, if you have a garden. You must be early due yourself, if you get ahead of the bugs. I think, that, on the whole, it would be best to sit up all night, and sleep daytimes. Things appear to go on in the night in the garden uncommonly. It would be less trouble to stay up than it is to get up so early.

E. A. Bowles
My Garden in Summer, 1914

It is fashionable nowadays to affect a horror of bedding plants. People say they must allow a few to please the gardener, just as they say they eat entrées and savouries to please the cook. The simple life is becoming an affectation in dinners and gardens; the table-cloth goes, but hard labour in polishing tables falls on the footmen, and even if you dine on a Tudor oak table you have a lace mat, and under that another fandangle, some bad conductor of heat for your plate to sit on. Simple? It reminds me of a silly old song that lilted of someone being as 'simple as Dahlias on Paddington Green.'

So we despise Scarlet Geraniums as we miscall our Zonal Pelargoniums, make a face at Calceolarias, and shudder at the mention of Blue Lobelia. Well, they have been sadly misused, I know, but they are fine plants, for all that, when in their right places. I remember a garden of twenty years ago that was the most bedded out I ever saw. Thousands of bedding plants were prepared for planting out in Summer, but always in straight lines in long, straight borders. It all began at the stable gates, and ran round three sides of the house, and continued in unbroken sequence, like Macbeth's vision of kings, for two sides of a croquet lawn, and then rushed up one side and down the other of a long path starting at right angles from the middle of the lawn, and if you began at the gates with Blue Lobelia, Mrs. Pollock Pelargonium, Perilla, Yellow Calceolaria, and some Scarlet Pelargonium in ranks according to their relative stature, so you continued for yards, poles, perches, furlongs, or whatever it was – I hate measures, and purposely forget them – and so you ended up when the border brought you back again to the lawn. I once suggested, Why not paint the ground in stripes, and have the effect all the year round, even if snow had to be swept off sometimes? I know an instance of a stately, formal garden which was found so expensive to fill with gay flowers that its owner had coloured tiles made to lay in the beds. Well, I do not champion that sort of thing, but I confess to adoring Scarlet Pelargoniums, rejoicing in Blue Lobelia, and revelling in Yellow Calceolaria. But they must be certain varieties, well grown and well placed. An aged Pelargonium, King of Denmark, with a tree-like trunk, numerous branches, and in a pot three sizes too small for it, can be a glorious cloud of warm salmon blossoms; and Paul Crampel is worth similar ill-treatment. Of course fat sappy cuttings stuck out in rich soil, and that grow leaves fit for cooking and serving with white sauce, are not what we want. I love to seize a few pot-plants in the conservatory or greenhouse, and to take them out for a Summer airing in the garden, sinking their pots among other plants, where they fit in and look as if they had been there all their lives. There is a raised bed near the house bordering the carriage drive that is getting filled up by degrees with permanent tenants, but among them at present are still a few lodgings to let, and here all sorts of tender plants pass their Summer. Yuccas form a large group at a corner, and next to them some grey-leaved things have gathered together. *Melianthus major* gets cut to the ground annually there, and retires under a heap of cinders we pile on it in November, but hitherto it has reappeared with Spring. *Senecio Greyi, S. compactus,* and *Othonnopis cheirifolia,* the Barbary Ragwort, sprawl down the bank. *Cineraria maritima* and *Centaurea Clementei* join their silvery forces to the others, and so work along till we reach a group of glaucous

Kniphofias such as *K. caulescens* and *K. Tysonii*. When Summer approaches it is very good fun to go into the houses and pick out certain things, to add to this mass of subtropical-looking foliage after they have had a week or so of hardening off. Purple-leaved Cannas are simply irresistible to group behind the Yuccas and the great ferny grey-leaves of *Melianthus major*. *Acacia Baileyana*, as blue as a freshly killed mackerel, can be slipped in among the Kniphofias and will tower above them. Blue Lobelia looks very lovely as a carpet spread among the feet of some of these, and a group of *Salvia patens*, that also has a poultice of ashes for Winter, is thereby kept in countenance and helps to make a patch of blue. Further along the bed we find a good place for sinking some large pots of *Moraea iridioides, M. bicolor* and *M. Huttonii*, as a low Yew hedge makes a good background for the yellow and black flowers of *bicolor*, and the white ones with mauve and orange trimmings of *iridioides*. This is a very curious Irid, and the only one I know of in which the flowering stem lives on for several years, branching out at intervals into green spathes and buds and flowers. Once an extra-industrious garden boy of a tidying-up disposition cut off all the old brown ugly stems at housing time, and of course for the next two years we had only a few flowers that the stems of the year could provide for us. The variety I have is the larger one sometimes known as *Dietes Macleai*, whose flowers are as large as those of *Iris unguicularis*, and much like them in general appearance and shape, pure glistening white with rich yellow keel to the falls, and lilac style branches. Each flower lasts about twenty-four hours only, but they are freely produced if unattacked by garden boys.

Mary Russell Mitford
Our Village, 1832

The pride of my heart and the delight of my eyes is my garden. Our house, which is in dimensions very much like a bird-cage, and might, with almost equal convenience, be laid on a shelf, or hung up in a tree, would be utterly unbearable in warm weather, were it not that we have a retreat out of doors – and a very pleasant retreat it is. To make my readers comprehend it, I must describe our whole territories.

Fancy a small plot of ground, with a pretty low irregular cottage at one end; a large granary, divided from the dwelling by a little court running along one side; and a long thatched shed, open towards the garden, and supported by wooden pillars, on the other. The bottom is bounded, half by an old wall, and half by an old paling, over which we see a pretty distance of woody hills. The house, granary, wall, and paling, are covered with vines, cherry-trees, roses, honeysuckles, and jessamines, with great clusters of tall hollyhocks running up between them; a large elder overhanging the little gate, and a magnificent bay-tree, such a tree as shall scarcely be matched in these parts, breaking with its beautiful conical form the horizontal lines of the buildings. This is my garden; and the long pillared shed, the sort of rustic arcade, which runs along one side, parted from the flower-beds by a row of rich geraniums, is our out-of-door drawing-room.

I know nothing so pleasant as to sit there on a summer afternoon, with the western sun flickering through the great elder-tree, and lighting up our gay

parterres, where flowers and flowering shrubs are set as thick as grass in a field, a wilderness of blossom, interwoven, intertwined, wreathy, garlandy, profuse beyond all profusion, where we may guess that there is such a thing as mould, but never see it. I know nothing so pleasant as to sit in the shade of that dark bower, with the eye resting on that bright piece of colour, lighted so gloriously by the evening sun, now catching a glimpse of the little birds as they fly rapidly in and out of their nests – for there are always two or three birds-nests in the thick tapestry of cherry-trees, honeysuckles, and China-roses, which covers our walls – now tracing the gay gambols of the common butterflies as they sport around the dahlias; now watching that rarer moth, which the country people, fertile in pretty names, call the bee-bird; that bird-like insect, which flutters in the hottest days over the sweetest flowers, inserting its long proboscis into the small tube of the jessamine, and hovering over the scarlet blossoms of the geranium, whose bright colour seems reflected on its own feathery breast: that insect which seems so thoroughly a creature of the air, never at rest; always, even when feeding, self-poised, and self-supported, and whose wings, in their ceaseless motion, have a sound so deep, so full, so lulling, so musical. Nothing so pleasant as to sit amid that mixture of the flower and the leaf, watching the bee-bird! Nothing so pretty to look at as my garden! It is quite a picture; only unluckily it resembles a picture in more qualities than one – it is fit for nothing but to look at. One might as well think of walking in a bit of framed canvass. There are walks to be sure – tiny paths of smooth gravel, by courtesy called such – but they are so overhung by roses and lilies, and such gay encroachers – so over-run by convolvulus, and heart's-ease, and mignonette, and other sweet stragglers, that, except to edge through them occasionally, for the purposes of planting, or weeding, or watering, there might as well be no paths at all. Nobody thinks of walking in my garden. Even May glides along with a delicate and trackless step, like a swan through the water; and we, its two-footed denizens, are fain to treat it as if it were really a saloon, and go out for a walk towards sun-set, just as if we had not been sitting in the open air all day.

Sir George Sitwell
On the Making of Gardens, 1909

Villa Torlonia at Frascati is not like Villa d'Este, where the great heart of the Anio throbs through the garden and every grove and thicket and alley is filled with a tumult of sobbing sound. It is a place of mysterious silence, of low-weeping fountains and muffled footfalls; a garden of sleep. The gates are on a lower level, and athwart the rose-tangled slope to the left the architect has thrown five great slanting staircases of stone, broad enough and splendid enough to carry an army of guests to the plateau above. But this is now a solitude, a mournful ilex *bosco* with cross walks and mossy fountains shaped like the baluster of some great sundial. From the central stairway, not far from the house, a broader opening in the woodland leads to a lawn and pool below the great cascade. In front is a long cliff crowned with ilex forest and faced with a frontispiece of moss-grown arches and bubbling fountains. The main fall drops from a balcony between two tall umbrageous ilexes which rise on either hand like the horns of an Addisonian periwig; from basin to basin it drops in a silver fringe, held in by low serpentine walls that curve and re-curve like the arches of a bridge or the edges of a shell. Through vaults on either hand, long winding stairways follow the curves, the masonry is choked with ferns, the steps with weeds, and riotous water-plants crowd upon the ledges or thrust green juicy stems through the scum which has gathered in the corners of the pools. At the top, in a small irregular clearing walled by wild ilex wood

and wilder tangle of flowering shrubs, is a balustraded basin in the form of a great *quatrefoil*. Gold-red fish gleam in the sea-green water, which reflects soft foliage and lichened stone and patches of pearly light; in the centre a huge cylinder of moss supports the silvery feathers of a fountain; it is an enchanted pool in a fairy woodland. But the traveller who has wandered here alone on a drowsy afternoon does not linger to listen to the trickle of the fountain and the murmuring of the bees. From below the threshold of the mind a strange sense of hidden danger oppresses him, an instinct neither to be reasoned with nor to be understood. Can there be brigands yet in the forest heights, or is the place haunted by shades of the soldiers who once fell in battle about the pool? He waits and wrestles with his folly, then sadly descending the slippery stairways leaves cooling fount and shaded alley for the torrid sunshine of the outer world.

It is death to sleep in the garden.

The great secret of success in garden-making [is] the profound platitude that we should abandon the struggle to make nature beautiful round the house and should rather move the house to where nature is beautiful. It is only part of the garden which lies within the boundary walls, and a great scheme planned for dull or commonplace surroundings is a faulty conception, as if one were to propose to build half a house or to paint half a picture. The garden must be considered not as a thing by itself, but as a gallery of foregrounds designed to set off the soft hues of the distance; it is nature which should call the tune, and the melody is to be found in the prospect of blue hill or shimmering lake, or mystery-haunted plain, in the aerial perspective of great trees beyond the boundary, in the green cliffs of leafy woodland which wall us in on either hand. It may be argued further that real beauty is neither in garden nor landscape, but in the relation of both to the individual, that what we are seeking is not only a scenic setting for pool and fountain and parterre, but a background for life. Natural loveliness at the doors will give a hundred times more enjoyment than loveliness a mile away, and as in the earlier days when every one's parlour was under the sky, when the heath and forest and moorland stretched up to the walls of the city and the towers of the castle, health will follow in its train. A garden in a verdurous landscape which strikes a note of beauty and freedom, of exuberant fertility, of happy adaptation to the service of man, will be a nobler gift to the future, more fitted to survive; we shall share in the overflowing happiness of others, and the halo of associations being so much a part of the self that the two can never be disentangled, those who are near to us will shine in our eyes with a reflected light.

William Morris
Hopes and Fears for Art, 1882

Our suburban gardeners in London, for instance, oftenest wind about their little bit of gravel walk and grass plot in ridiculous imitation of an ugly big garden of the landscape gardening style, and then with a strange perversity fill up the spaces with the most formal plants they can get; whereas the merest common-sense should have taught them to lay out their morsel of ground in the simplest way, to fence it as orderly as might be, one part from the other – if it be big enough for that – and the whole from the road, and then to fill up the flower-growing space with things that are free and interesting in their growth, leaving Nature to do the desired complexity, which she will certainly not fail to do, if we do not desert her for the florist, who, I must say, has made it harder work than it should be to get the best of flowers. . . .

As to colour in gardens. Flowers in masses are mighty strong colour, and if not used with a great deal of caution are very destructive to pleasure in gardening. On the whole, I think the best and safest plan is to mix up your flowers, and rather eschew great masses of colour – in combination, I mean. But there are some flowers – inventions of men, *i.e.* florists – which are bad colour altogether, and not to be used at all. Scarlet geraniums, for instance, or the yellow calceolaria, which, indeed, are not uncommonly grown together profusely, in order, I suppose, to show that even flowers can be thoroughly ugly.

And now to sum up as to a garden. Large or small, it should look both orderly and rich. It should be well fenced from the outside world. It should by no means imitate either the wilfulness or the wildness of Nature, but should look like a thing never to be seen except near a house. It should, in fact, look like a part of the house. It follows from this that no private pleasure-garden should be very big, and a public garden should be divided and made to look like so many flower-closes in a meadow, or a wood, or amidst the pavement.

It will be a key to right thinking about gardens if you will consider in what kind of places a garden is most desired. In a very beautiful country, especially if it be mountainous, we can do without it well enough; whereas in a flat and dull country we crave after it, and there it is often the very making of the homestead. While in great towns, gardens, both private and public, are positive necessities if the citizens are to live reasonable and healthy lives in body and mind.

Reginald Farrer
The English Rock Garden, 1919

It is impossible to codify cast-iron rules for the successful cultivation of each plant. Only the fool or the tiro dogmatises; the further one progresses in knowledge, the more certain one grows of one's ignorance. The small, faint, illuminated patch of our experience only shows up the vast darkness by which our little islet of light is surrounded, and makes it seem yet smaller by comparison. General rules for cultivation have already been abundantly propounded; and it must never be forgotten that the enormous majority of alpine plants require no more. At the same time I have also given a general sketch of the conditions under which they grow in nature, not because it is by any means desirable to copy these with slavish precision, but because, from the native circumstances of its success, the enthusiast will soon be able to divine the riddle of each plant's personality and act accordingly. It would be idle waste of labour to attempt any precise imitation of the natural conditions under which a given species thrives; silly, because impossible adequately to do so – idle, because very probably it will thrive quite as well, if not indeed much better, under quite different ones. Sea-sand plants, for instance, are often luxuriant in common loam, and many an alpine is fat and happy in the ordinary border. It is only as a resource of despair and a confession of failure, after all other experiments have failed, that one tries to achieve some empirical reproduction of its native circumstances, in the case of an

especially difficult and recalcitrant treasure. Otherwise, though study of a plant's normal surroundings is of acute interest and value, it should be undertaken chiefly as a means of detecting the plant's own character; and estimated, like the Apocrypha, as an ensample of right living, but not as in any way essential to horticultural salvation.

Canon Henry Ellacombe
In a Gloucestershire Garden, 1896

There is plenty of work in the garden in November, and in its way very interesting, the more so because it is unlike the work of any other month. We may lament the loss of leaves on the trees, and the change in them from thick masses of green to bare skeletons. But these skeletons have a beauty of their own, and to the botanist and student of tree-life they are a very pleasant study; indeed, no one can venture on a record of the life of a tree or shrub who does not as much study its anatomy in the winter as he does the leaves, flowers, and fruits in the summer. The anatomy of trees is a constant marvel, and to study it thoroughly will teach many unexpected lessons: to mark the different angles and thicknesses of the branches, varying in every tree according to the necessities of each family and each species, and varying in trees of the same species according to their position as regards light and soil and prevailing winds, will require many a winter's study. And in November, when the trees are bare of leaves, is the time for that pruning of trees which is one of the pleasantest labours of the garden, and one of the most healthy; but it is an art that is not soon learned, and in no branch of gardening does experience and steady observation of the wants and growth of trees produce better results. A tree that has been well looked after from its infancy will show a vigour both in girth and height over neglected trees that will be a surprise to many, and a good object-lesson to those who think that everything may be left to nature.

Another very pleasant November work is the carrying out alterations in the garden, including the removal of all sorts of plants. I am in the habit during the summer of making notes of work to be done in the winter, such as the removal of plants which are getting too crowded, or which are evidently not happy in their present position, or the alteration of paths and beds made necessary by the growth of trees, or it may be merely by the desire for change; and all such work is best done in November. In some gardens there is a great deal of work done in the separation of plants, and I know of many who think that frequent separation is absolutely necessary to the well-being of plants. It may be so in some soils, especially in heavy clay soils, but I am glad that it is not necessary for me. I find it better to leave plants alone as much as possible; there are some which from time to time I may be obliged to divide, but I do it unwillingly, for I find, in many cases, that it takes them more than a year to recover from the operation. This is especially the case with roses, lilies, and pæonies, but I believe this is entirely a question of soil, and what is a law for my garden is no law for

others. In my own garden I am not afraid of moving plants at almost any time of the year, if I see the necessity for it; but to move plants in the height of summer requires extra care in planting, and much watching after planting; in November the work is much easier. There are few gardening works in which a gardener's skill, or want of skill, are more shown than in removing plants from one place to another, especially shrubs; and in no branch are there so many disappointments when the work is done by careless or unskilful hands. All that such trees or shrubs ask for is that they should be kept out of the ground as short a time as possible, and be placed in their new home very firmly; and, to get this firmness, a few heavy stones placed near the stem are a good help, they prevent the plant being much swayed by the wind, and they prevent the evaporation of moisture and the loss of warmth by radiation. . . .

I have always noticed that the more a man loves his garden, the more he delights in constantly changing the arrangements, which were, perhaps, good for a time, but which, as time goes on, must give way to others; and the most uninteresting garden is one that has been made on a fixed plan, rigidly adhered to through succeeding years, till what may have been good and beautiful at the beginning becomes dull, uninteresting, and ugly. Personally, I have little faith in fixed plans, perhaps because I have never had any plan in my own garden; such as it is, it has grown into its present shape and plan, and has almost formed itself; and I may say with certainty that though I have many trees, shrubs, and other plants which have been in their present places for many years – many over seventy years – yet there is not a single path or flower-bed that is the same now as it was thirty or even twenty years ago. And this adds much to the pleasure of a garden; this power of altering to suit the wants of growing trees and shrubs, or it may be only to suit one's own peculiar taste or fancy, gives a pleasant feeling of ownership which nothing else will give.

Eleanour Sinclair Rohde
The Scented Garden, 1931

It is curious how the same flower scent affects people differently according to circumstances. The scent of gorse flowers, especially of the double flowered gorse, would not, I think, give us much pleasure in summer, yet in spring it seems to hold captive as by a miracle the glory of a whole day of sun and warmth. The rather crude scent of cow-parsley in mass is not a favourite scent with country-folk. But to town-folk it is delightful, simply because it is one of the most familiar scents of an English lane in May. To anyone returning from a tropical country it is probably far more welcome than any rich Eastern scent, and for no other reason than that it is one of the homely country smells with which he has been familiar from childhood. Few people appreciate the scent of broad bean flowers, simply because the broad bean is a 'vegetable,' yet it is one of the most beautiful of flower scents. Broad beans are usually regarded as the only 'vegetable' with scented flowers, but sea-kale flowers have almost as attractive a scent, for although less sweet it is nut-like and mellower. The only other 'vegetables' with scented attractions are, I think, the delicate morel mushrooms, which appear very early in the year, and have a most pleasant scent. The scent of elder, when one encounters it on the highway, is 'heady' and overpowering, but in a hayfield, when it blends with the newly-mown hay curing in the sun, it is a pleasant smell. Meadowsweet in the mass is a dull and rather heavy smell, but if one is in a boat and the scent is wafted by a passing breeze across water this perfume is sweet, and suggestive of the fulness and richness of summer. The smell of the peppermint plants by the stream-side, crushed by the boat against the river bank, is also pleasantest when water-borne. To town-dwellers the scent of hay in haymaking time must be almost unbearable, for surely no other smell makes them realize with the same poignancy that their lot is that of prisoners, no matter how gilded their cages may be. For the scent of hay in all its stages is one of those all-pervading primitive scents of which it is more true to say that one is enfolded in it rather than that one smells it. Even a whiff of hay scent from a passing cart in a city has a magical effect, for the street disappears and one sees instead the shimmering heat in the hayfield at noonday, the hedgerow starred with wild roses and the first bramble flowers, the butterflies flitting to and fro, the lowly many-hued undergrowth of daisies, lady's bedstraw and trefoil and tufted vetch in the depths of the sea of grass. Sweetest of all is meadow hay. The scent of a newly-made stack is fresh, but the scent of an old stack has perhaps the finer aroma. . . .

Fragrance in flowers may, indeed, be described as their music, and it is none the less beautiful because it is silent. In every scented flower and leaf the perfume is exhaled by substances so perfectly blended that they give the impression of a single scent, just as several different notes make a chord. We are all familiar with the dual sensation produced by smelling any sweet-scented flower – both an appreciation of the perfume and the still deeper pleasure afforded by something so delicately balanced and, as it were, faultlessly rounded that it seems almost beyond our mere human senses to enjoy it fully.

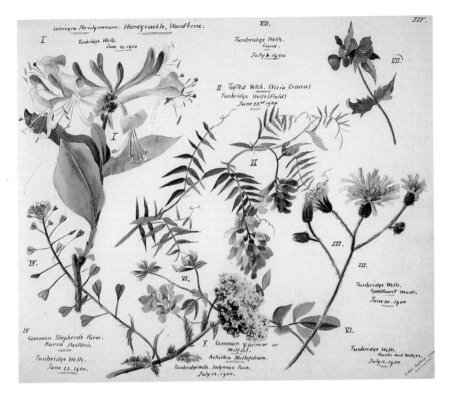

S. Reynolds Hole
A Book about the Garden and the Gardener, 1909

Recall the charming diversity of colour and of form which they, the annuals, perennials, and bulbous plants of spring, present to our admiration. Of form, from the tall imperial fritillaria, having the resemblance of crown and of sceptre also, to the prostrate stonecrop, carpeting the ground beneath. Of colour, what a range, what a rich variety! All colours, primary and intermediate, brilliant and soft, positive and neutral – colours to harmonize, colours to contrast, the colours which I like, and the colours which you like – all of them are here. Does your eye delight in the glow and brightness of the more vivid tints? Look at that anemone, well-named 'fulgens,' all afire in crimson glory! Regard these tulips – General Garibaldi, in his scarlet uniform, or royally named and royally apparelled, rex rubrorum, the King of the Reds! Gaze upon that gentian (the vernal), luminous, gleaming like the breast of a humming-bird with an intense and dazzling blue! Watch that clump of the yellow crocus, as they open to receive the kisses of the sun (if any); and what is there in the stove, or even in the summer-garden, in orchid, allamanda, or calceolaria, which can vie with them in their golden sheen?

Or have you what is called a more 'quiet taste'? Bend over this bed of myosotis dissitiflora, bluer than the turquoise, blue as the heavens, and you need not ask from the gardener, or search in floral dictionary, a translation of the name, for the flower itself speaks it in your ear, and whispers, 'forget-

me-not.' Or turn to that patch of the exquisite, dainty little scillas . . . or to that sheet of roseate silene, blue mountain-anemone, purple pansy, pale yellow primrose, bright yellow cheiranthus, lilac aubrietia, or (yet more appropriate to one who is talking of sheets) to those snow-white masses of candytuft (iberis correæfolia is the fairest of the fair), of alyssum, arabis, saxifrage, daisy, and snowdrop.

J. C. Loudon
'Calls in Hertfordshire, Bedfordshire, Berkshire, Surrey, Sussex and Middlesex', 1833

At Mortimer Street, the vicarage house has a very beautiful flower-garden and shrubbery, with a piece of water, the beauty of which may be fully enjoyed by passengers on the road. The grounds consist of two banks of turf which slope down to the pond, and the whole is considerably below the eye of a person walking along the road. It would be easy to shut it out by a hedge of ordinary height, but we recommend the taste and good feeling of the proprietor, in wishing his neighbours and the public to participate in his enjoyments. We know nothing of this vicar, not even his name; but we have little doubt that he is a good man. It seems to us that every man, in ornamenting his house, his garden, or his estate, however small it may be, ought to consider not only his own gratification, but the ornament and benefit of his country. He ought always to ask himself, what the passers by will think of what he is doing.

William Robinson
The Wild Garden, 1870

Not to mow is almost a necessity in the wild garden, and as there is often in large gardens much more mown surface than is necessary, many will not regret it. Here the Grass is left unmown in many places. Of course it may be cut when ripe, and most of the spring flowers have past and their leaves are out of danger. Even in parts where no flowers are planted the Grass is left till long enough to cut as meadow. Except where wanted as a carpet, Grass may often be allowed to grow even in the pleasure ground; quite as good an effect is afforded by unmown as the mown Grass – indeed, better when the long Grass is full of flowers. Three-fourths of the most lovely flowers of cold and temperate regions are companions of the Grass – like Grasses in hardiness, like Grasses in summer life and winter rest, like Grasses in stature. Whatever plants may seem best to associate together in gardens, an immense number – more than two thousand species of those now cultivated – would thrive to perfection among our meadow Grasses, as they do on the Grassy breast of the mountain in many northern lands. Some, like the tall Irises or Columbines, will show their heads clear above the delicate bloom of the Grass; others, like the Cerastiums, will open their cups below it. The varieties of Columbine in the Grass were perhaps the prettiest flowers at the time of my visit. The white, purplish, and delicately-coloured forms of this charming old plant, just seen above the tops of the long Grass, growing singly, in little groups, or in colonies, formed a June

ALFRED PARSONS
1880

garden of themselves. Established among the Grass, they will henceforward, like it, take care of themselves. The rosy, heart-shaped blooms of the Dielytra spectabilis are seen at some distance through the Grass, and, so grown, furnish a bright and pretty effect. Tree Pæonies succeed, and their great heads of flower quite light up this charming wilderness. Plants of the Goat's Beard Spiræa (S. Aruncus) are very stately and graceful, even now, before they flower, being quite 6 feet high. In the wild garden, apart from the naturalization of free-growing exotics, the establishment of rare British flowers is one of the most interesting occupations; and here, under a Pine tree, the modest, trailing Linnæa borealis of the northern Fir-woods is beginning to spread. The Fox-glove was not originally found in the neighbourhood; now the ordinary kind and the various other forms of this fine wild flower adorn the woods. In this way also the Lily of the Valley has been planted and is spreading rapidly. Many climbing Roses and various other climbers have been planted at the bases of trees and stumps. A White Indian Clematis here, first trained on a wall, sent up some of its shoots through a tree close at hand, and now the long shoots hang from the tree full of flowers. The large plumes of the nobler hardy Ferns are seen here and there through the trees and Grass, and they are better here among the Grass and flowers, half shaded by trees, than in the 'hardy Fernery.' The wild garden of the future will be also the true home of all the larger hardy Ferns. The rivals of the Ferns in beauty of foliage, the Ferulas, and other hardy plants with beautifully cut foliage, have also their homes in the wild garden. The Welsh Poppy thrives, as might be expected, admirably in the grove, its rich yellow cups just showing above the meadow.

In another part of the grounds there is a high walk quite away from trees, open and dry, with banks on each side – a sun-walk, with Scotch Roses,

Brooms, Sun Roses, Rock Roses, and things that love the sun, like the plants of the hot and rocky hillsides of the Mediterranean shores. Spanish Broom, Lavenders, Rosemary, Thyme, and Balm, are among the plants that thrive as well on a sunny sandy bank in England as in Italy or Greece.

True taste in the garden is, unhappily, much rarer than many people suppose. No amount of expense, rich collections, good cultivation, large gardens, and plenty of glass, will suffice. A garden of a few acres showing a real love of the beautiful in Nature, as it can be illustrated in gardens, is rare; and when it is seen it is often rather the result of accident than of design. This is partly owing to the fact that the kind of knowledge one wants in order to form a really beautiful garden is very uncommon. No man can do so with few materials. It is necessary to have some knowledge of the wealth of beauty which the world contains for our gardens; and yet this knowledge must not have a leaning, or at any rate but a very partial leaning, towards the Dryasdust. The disposition to 'dry' everything, to concern oneself entirely with nomenclature and classification, is not the gardening spirit – it is the *life* we want.

Reginald Blomfield
The Formal Garden in England, 1892

The landscape gardener attempts to establish a sort of hierarchy of nature, based on much the same principle as that which distinguishes a gentleman by his incapacity to do any useful work. Directly it is proved that a plant or a tree is good for food, it is expelled from the flower garden without any regard to its intrinsic beauty. The hazel-hedge has gone, and the apple-tree has long been banished from the flowers. Of all the trees an apple-tree in full bloom, or ripe in autumn, is perhaps the loveliest. Trained as an espalier it makes a beautiful hedge, and set out as in an orchard it lets the sun play through its leaves and chequer with gold the green velvet of the grass in a way that no other tree will quite allow. Nothing can be more beautiful than some of the walks under the apple-trees in the gardens at Penshurst. Yet the landscape gardener would shudder at the idea of planting a grove or hedge of apple-trees in his garden. Instead of this he will give you a conifer or a monkey-puzzler, though the guelder-rose grows wild in the meadow and the spindle-tree in the wood, and the rowan, the elder, and the white-thorn; and the wild cherry in autumn fires the woodland with its crimson and gold. Every one admires these as a matter of proper sensibility to nature, but it does not seem to occur to people that they would grow with as little difficulty in a garden, and at the very smallest expense. It would undoubtedly injure the business of the nursery gardener to allow that they were possible. Again, the pear-tree and the chequer-tree, the quince, the medlar, and the mulberry are surely entitled by their beauty to a place in the garden. It is only since nature has been taken in hand by the landscapist and taught her proper position that these have been excluded. When there was no talk about nature, and man had not learnt to consider himself as something detached from nature and altogether superior, the fruit tree was counted among the beauties of the garden. . . . It is more of this unsophisticated liking for everything that is beautiful that ought to be allowed full play in the gardens; less of the pedantry that lays down rules about nature and is at heart indifferent to the beauty about which it preaches. . . .

A garden is so much an individual affair – it should show so distinctly the idiosyncrasy of its owner – that it would be useless to offer any hints as to its details. . . . The characteristic of the old formal garden, the garden of Markham and Lawson, was its exceeding simplicity. The primary purpose of a garden as a place of retirement and seclusion, a place for quiet thought and leisurely enjoyment, was kept steadily in view. The grass and the yew trees were trimmed close to gain their full beauty from the sunlight. Sweet kindly flowers filled the knots and borders. Peacocks and pigeons brightened the terraces and lawns. The paths were straight and ample, the garden-house solidly built and comfortable; everything was reasonable and unaffected. But this simple genuine delight in nature and art became feebler as the seventeenth century grew older. Gardening became the fashionable art, and this was the golden age for professional gardeners; but the real pleasure of it was gone. Rows of statues were introduced from the French, costly architecture superseded the simple terrace, intricate parterres were laid out from gardeners' pattern books, and meanwhile the flowers were forgotten. It was well that all this pomp should be swept away.

Henry David Thoreau
Walden, 1854

Meanwhile my beans, the length of whose rows, added together, was seven miles already planted, were impatient to be hoed, for the earliest had grown considerably before the latest were in the ground; indeed they were not easily to be put off. What was the meaning of this so steady and self-respecting, this small Herculean labor, I knew not. I came to love my rows, my beans, though so many more than I wanted. They attached me to the earth, and so I got strength like Antæus. But why should I raise them? Only Heaven knows. This was my curious labor all summer – to make this portion of the earth's surface, which had yielded only cinquefoil, blackberries, johnswort, and the like, before, sweet wild fruits and pleasant flowers, produce instead this pulse. What shall I learn of beans or beans of me? I cherish them, I hoe them, early and late I have an eye to them; and this is my day's work. It is a fine broad leaf to look on. My auxiliaries are the dews and rains which water this dry soil, and what fertility is in the soil itself, which for the most part is lean and effete. My enemies are worms, cool days, and most of all woodchucks. The last have nibbled for me a quarter of an acre clean. But what right had I to oust johnswort and the rest, and break up their ancient herb garden? Soon, however, the remaining beans will be too tough for them, and go forward to meet new foes. . . .

It was a singular experience that long acquaintance which I cultivated with beans, what with planting, and hoeing, and harvesting, and threshing,

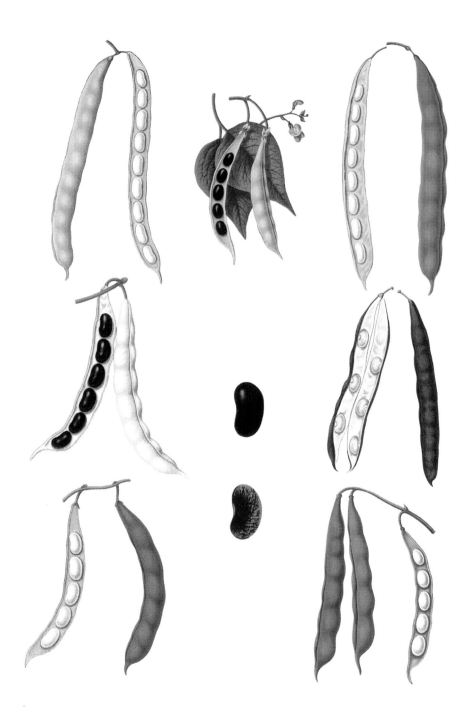

and picking over and selling them – the last was the hardest of all – I might add eating, for I did taste. I was determined to know beans. When they were growing, I used to hoe from five o'clock in the morning till noon, and commonly spent the rest of the day about other affairs. Consider the intimate and curious acquaintance one makes with various kinds of weeds – it will bear some iteration in the account, for there was no little iteration in the labor – disturbing their delicate organizations so ruthlessly, and making such invidious distinctions with his hoe, levelling whole ranks of one species, and sedulously cultivating another. That's Roman wormwood – that's pigweed – that's sorrel – that's piper-grass – have at him, chop him up, turn his roots upward to the sun, don't let him have a fibre in the shade, if you do he'll turn himself t' other side up and be as green as a leek in two days. A long war, not with cranes, but with weeds, those Trojans who had sun and rain and dews on their side. Daily the beans saw me come to their rescue armed with a hoe, and thin the ranks of their enemies, filling up the trenches with weedy dead. Many a lusty crest-waving Hector, that towered a whole foot above his crowding comrades, fell before my weapon and rolled in the dust.

Those summer days which some of my contemporaries devoted to the fine arts in Boston or Rome, and others to contemplation in India, and others to trade in London or New York, I thus, with the other farmers of New England, devoted to husbandry. Not that I wanted beans to eat, for I am by nature a Pythagorean, so far as beans are concerned, whether they mean porridge or voting, and exchanged them for rice; but, perchance, as some must work in fields if only for the sake of tropes and expression, to serve a parable-maker one day. It was on the whole a rare amusement, which, continued too long, might have become a dissipation. Though I gave them no manure, and did not hoe them all once, I hoed them unusually well as far as I went, and was paid for it in the end, 'there being in truth,' as Evelyn says, 'no compost or laetation whatsoever comparable to this continual motion, repastination, and turning of the mould with the spade.' 'The earth,' he adds elsewhere, 'especially if fresh, has a certain magnetism in it, by which it attracts the salt, power, or virtue (call it either) which gives it life, and is the logic of all the labor and stir we keep about it, to sustain us; all dungings and other sordid temperings being but the vicars succedaneous to this improvement.' Moreover, this being one of those 'worn-out and exhausted lay fields which enjoy their sabbath,' had perchance, as Sir Kenelm Digby thinks likely, attracted 'vital spirits' from the air. I harvested twelve bushels of beans.

Lewis Carroll
Through the Looking Glass, 1872

This time she came upon a large flower-bed, with a border of daisies, and a willow-tree growing in the middle.

'O Tiger-lily,' said Alice, addressing herself to one that was waving gracefully about in the wind, 'I *wish* you could talk!'

'We *can* talk,' said the Tiger-lily: 'when there's anybody worth talking to.'

Alice was so astonished that she couldn't speak for a minute: it quite seemed to take her breath away. At length, as the Tiger-lily only went on waving about, she spoke again, in a timid voice – almost in a whisper. 'And can *all* the flowers talk?'

'As well as *you* can,' said the Tiger-lily. 'And a great deal louder.'

'It isn't manners for us to begin, you know,' said the Rose, 'and I really was wondering when you'd speak! Said I to myself: "Her face has got *some* sense in it, though it's not a clever one!" Still you're the right colour, and that goes a long way.'

'I don't care about the colour,' the Tiger-lily remarked. 'If only her petals curled up a little more, she'd be all right.'

Alice didn't like being criticised, so she began asking questions: 'Aren't you sometimes frightened at being planted out here, with nobody to take care of you?'

'There's the tree in the middle,' said the Rose.

'What else is it good for?'

'But what could it do, if any danger came?' Alice asked.

'It could bark,' said the Rose.

'It says "Bough-wough," cried a Daisy: 'that's why its branches are called boughs!'

'Didn't you know *that?*' cried another Daisy, and here they all began shouting together, till the air seemed quite full of little shrill voices.

'Silence, every one of you!' cried the Tiger-lily, waving itself passionately from side to side, and trembling with excitement. 'They know I can't get at them!' it panted, bending its quivering head towards Alice, 'or they wouldn't dare do it!'

'Never mind!' Alice said in a soothing tone, and stooping down to the daisies, who were just beginning again, she whispered, 'If you don't hold your tongues, I'll pick you!'

There was silence in a moment, and several of the pink daisies turned white.

'That's right!' said the Tiger-lily. 'The daisies are worst of all. When one speaks, they all begin together, and it's enough to make one wither to hear the way they go on!'

'How is it you can all talk so nicely?' Alice said, hoping to get it into a better temper by a compliment. 'I've been in many gardens before, but none of the flowers could talk.'

'Put your hand down, and feel the ground,' said the Tiger-lily. 'Then you'll know why.'

Alice did so. 'It's very hard,' she said, 'but I don't see what that has to do with it.'

'In most gardens,' the Tiger-lily said, 'they make the beds too soft – so that the flowers are always asleep.'

This sounded a very good reason, and Alice was quite pleased to know it. 'I never thought of that before!' she said.

'It's *my* opinion you never think *at all*,' the Rose said in a rather severe tone.

'I never saw anybody that looked stupider,' a Violet said, so suddenly, that Alice quite jumped; for it hadn't spoken before.

'Hold *your* tongue!' cried the Tiger-lily. 'As if *you* ever saw anybody! You keep your head under the leaves, and snore away there till you know no more what's going on in the world, than if you were a bud!'

J. M. Synge

'A Landlord's Garden in County Wicklow'
In Wicklow and West Kerry, 1912

A stone's throw from an old house where I spent several summers in County Wicklow, there was a garden that had been left to itself for fifteen or twenty years. Just inside the gate, as one entered, two paths led up through a couple of strawberry beds, half choked with leaves, where a few white and narrow strawberries were still hidden away. Further on was nearly half an acre of tall raspberry canes and thistles five feet high, growing together in a dense mass, where one could still pick raspberries enough to last a household for the season. Then, in a waste of hemlock, there were some half-dozen apple trees covered with lichen and moss, and against the northern walls a few dying plum trees hanging from their nails. Beyond them there was a dead pear tree, and just inside the gate, as one came back to it, a large fuchsia filled with empty nests. A few lines of box here and there showed where the flower-beds had been laid out, and when anyone who had the knowledge looked carefully among them many remnants could be found of beautiful and rare plants.

All round this garden there was a wall seven or eight feet high, in which one could see three or four tracks with well-worn holes – like the paths down a cliff in Kerry – where boys and tramps came over to steal and take away any apples or other fruits that were in season. Above the wall on the three windy sides there were rows of finely-grown lime trees, the place of meeting in the summer for ten thousand bees. Under the east wall there was the roof of a green-house, where one could sit, when it was wet or dry, and watch the birds and butterflies, many of which were not common. The seasons were always late in this place – it was high above the sea – and redpoles often used to nest not far off late in the summer; siskins did the same once or twice, and greenfinches, till the beginning of August, used to cackle endlessly in the lime trees.

Frances Hodgson Burnett
The Secret Garden, 1911

It was the sweetest, most mysterious-looking place any one could imagine. The high walls which shut it in were covered with the leafless stems of climbing roses which were so thick that they were matted together. Mary Lennox knew they were roses because she had seen a great many roses in India. All the ground was covered with grass of a wintry brown and out of it grew clumps of bushes which were surely rosebushes if they were alive.

There were numbers of standard roses which had so spread their branches that they were like little trees. There were other trees in the garden, and one of the things which made the place look strangest and loveliest was that climbing roses had run all over them and swung down long tendrils which made light swaying curtains, and here and there they had caught at each other or at a far-reaching branch and had crept from one tree to another and made lovely bridges of themselves. There were neither leaves nor roses on them now and Mary did not know whether they were dead or alive, but their thin gray or brown branches and sprays looked like a sort of hazy mantle spreading over everything, walls, and trees, and even brown grass, where they had fallen from their fastenings and run along the ground. It was this hazy tangle from tree to tree which made it all look so mysterious. Mary had thought it must be different from other gardens which had not

been left all by themselves so long; and indeed it was different from any other place she had ever seen in her life.

'How still it is!' she whispered. 'How still!'

Then she waited a moment and listened at the stillness. The robin, who had flown to his treetop, was still as all the rest. He did not even flutter his wings; he sat without stirring, and looked at Mary.

'No wonder it is still,' she whispered again. 'I am the first person who has spoken in here for ten years.'

E. H. Wilson
Plant Hunting, 1927

The road [from Sungpang Ting] is narrow; sometimes it skirts the edge of the river's turbulent waters but more usually ribbon-like it winds along from fifty to 300 feet above. The passing of mule-trains is a difficult business, often possible only at particular places when one caravan comes to a stand-still and allows the other to pass.

I travelled mostly on foot but had with me a light sedan chair made of rattan and my Boy or principal servant was similarly favored. A sedan chair is an outward and visible sign of respectability without which no traveller is properly equipped. In those days it was of far more importance than a passport, for it inspired confidence and insured the respect of the people. Whether one rode in it or walked was immaterial; the important thing was its presence.

On the seventh day we were down to 5500 feet altitude and the following extract from my diary seems worth recording: 'A bad road through barren, desolate country and abnormally long miles sums up the day's journey. Barring absolute desert no more barren and repelling country could be imagined than that traversed today. But it is really only the narrow valley and precipitous mountain-sides that are so desert-like. On the upper slopes trees and cultivation occur and small villages and farmhouses are frequent. In the valley houses are far between and what few there are are in ruinous condition. A fierce up-river wind blows regularly from about eleven o'clock in the morning and it is difficult to make headway against it. The leaves on the Maize plants are torn to shreds by the wind's violence. The houses are of mud and flat-roofed, as protection against the winds. The Regal Lily occurs here and there in abundance on the well-nigh stark slate and mudstone cliffs.'

The eighth day I camped and for several days was busy arranging to secure in October, the proper season of the year, some six or seven thousand bulbs of the Regal Lily. Plans completed we set out for Chengtu Fu, the capital city of Szechuan. The hardship of a four months' journey were beginning to tell on me and dysentery in a mild form had troubled me for days. Yet it was with a light heart and a satisfied mind that I rode in my chair. Soon after starting we passed a mule-train breaking camp and bound our way. With the thoughts of the flesh pots of Chengtu Fu only four days' distance, all were in a cheerful mood. We were making good progress, my chair leading, with personal attendants and man carrying my large camera immediately behind; my black spaniel dog wagging his tail ahead of us all. The Chinese characters of warning carved in the rocks did not afright us, we had seen so many and passed all well. Song was in our hearts, when I noticed my dog suddenly cease wagging his tail, cringe and rush forward and a small piece of rock hit the path and rebounded into the river some 300 feet below us. I shouted an order and the bearers put down the chair. The two front bearers ran forward and I essayed to follow suit. Just as I cleared the chair-handles a large boulder crashed into the body of the chair and down to the river it was hurled. I ran, instinctively ducked as something whisked over my head and my sun hat blew off. Again I ran, a few yards more and I would be under the lea of some hard rocks. Then feeling as if a hot wire passed through my leg, I was bowled over, tried to

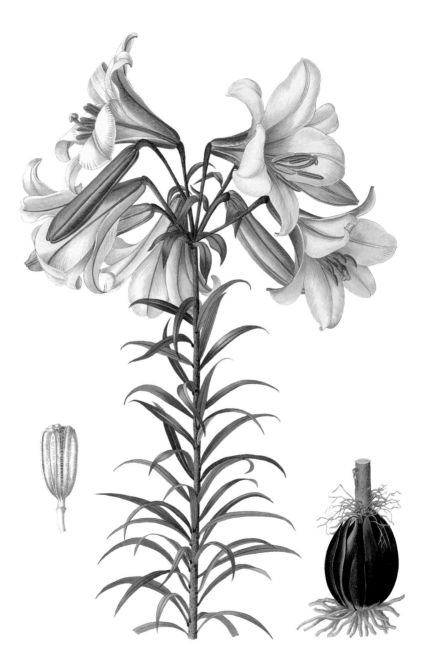

jump up, found my right leg was useless, so crawled forward to the shelter of the cliff, where the two scared chair-bearers were huddled.

It was only a small slide and our lives had had a providential escape. The man carrying my camera could not run back so fast as others and suffered a bad scalp wound. I was the biggest sufferer but, fortunately, was not knocked unconscious. If I had been the men would probably have deserted from fright, as it was they behaved well. The pigskin puttee on my right leg was cut slantingly as with a knife and forced round my leg, the toe cap of my boot was torn off and with it the nail of my big toe; the right leg was broken in two places below the knee and the side of my calf was badly lacerated. Not a pleasant situation to find oneself in alone with Chinese and four days from the nearest medical assistance!

As soon as it was safe to do so the men came along, terrified and solicitous. My Boy with his chair also came soon afterward but was quite ignorant of the whole affair. With the legs of my camera tripod I improvised splints and while these were being bandaged to my leg the mule-caravan passed in the morning loomed into view. The road was too narrow for them to turn back and they dare not stand still until I could be moved forward, since we knew not when the rock slide would re-commence. There was only one thing to do. I lay across the road and the mules stepped over my body. Then it was that I realized the size of the mule's hoof. There were nearer fifty than forty of them and each stepped clearly over me as if accustomed to such obstacles. Nevertheless, I breathed freely when the last was over!

IV

VOICES AMONG US

It is quite impossible to characterize garden writing today with a phrase or two. In Michael Pollan and Eleanor Perényi we have pungent and amusing commentators on the process of gardening and the natural world. There are experts like Christopher Lloyd, prepared to guide us with style and precision through the subtleties of the art. Humorists Beverley Nichols and Henry Mitchell would be fun to read on any subject, and all the more so writing about something they – and we – love. Karel Čapek, writing in Czech more than seventy years ago, is somehow able to strike through to the very essence of gardening as we all know it right now. Anna Pavord, Vita Sackville-West, Russell Page – each is distinctive, each has something fascinating to say, and each deserves a place in the pantheon. Gardeners who like to read are indeed blessed.

Gertrude Jekyll
Home and Garden, 1900

Leading to the Wall-flower garden I should like to have a way between narrow rock borders or dry walls. These should be planted with Aubretias, varieties of *A. græca*, of full and light purple colour, and a good quantity of the grey foliage and tender white bloom of *Cerastium tomentosum*, so common in gardens and yet so seldom well used: I would also have, but more sparingly, the all-pervading *Arabis albida*.

These plants, with the exception of the Cuckoo-flower, are among the most often found in gardens, but it is very rarely that they are used thoughtfully or intelligently, or in such a way as to produce the simple pictorial effect to which they so readily lend themselves. This planting of white and purple colouring I would back with plants or shrubs of dark foliage, and the path should be so directed into the Wall-flower garden, by passing through a turn or a tunnelled arch of Yew or some other dusky growth, that one is not seen from the other; but so that the eye, attuned to the cold, fresh colouring of the white and purple, should be in the very best state to receive and enjoy the sumptuous splendour of the region beyond. I am not sure that the return journey would not present the more brilliant picture of the two, for I have often observed in passing from warm colouring to cold, that the eye receives a kind of delightful shock of surprise that colour can be so strong and so pure and so altogether satisfying. And in these ways one gets to know how to use colour to the

Arabis Turrita   *Tower Wall Cress*

best garden effects. It is a kind of optical gastronomy; this preparation and presentation of food for the eye in arrangements that are both wholesome and agreeable, and in which each course is so designed that it is the best possible preparation for the next one to come.

Christopher Lloyd
The Well-Tempered Garden, 1970

Many gardeners will agree that hand-weeding is not the terrible drudgery that it is often made out to be. Some people find in it a kind of soothing monotony. It leaves their minds free to develop the plot for their next novel or to perfect the brilliant repartee with which they should have countered a relative's latest example of unreasonableness.

Efficient hand-weeding requires that you should get down to the task on your knees: as comfortably as possible, with a soft rubber mat and a good sharp-pointed, sharp-edged, stainless steel trowel.

You will observe that professional gardeners do all hand-weeding from a standing stooping position. They pull the weeds out (or break them off) by the hair and do not use a trowel. Their standards of weeding are mediocre, but they remain men, standing proudly, if not erect, at least on their two feet, whereas you and I become animals, even reptiles. The one advantage that I must give the standing posture (having no inhibitions about crawling on all fours) is that it occupies the least lateral space and is hence less damaging, in close country.

If you are working from a path, there are no problems: but if you are burrowing into and among plants in a border, you should do as much as you can from one position, because the more often you move, the more havoc is your frame likely to wreak. So you should be sufficiently ambidextrous to be able to wield the trowel with either hand, collecting up

199

the weeds with the other. Some weeds are notoriously wet, even in dry weather – opium poppies and chickweed in particular – so that the collecting hand gets clogged with slime and mud. Given a change of job, as trowel manipulator, it will soon dry out.

Of recent years I have had to take to gardening in gloves because of skin allergies. I never thought I could weed with gloves on. 'I must be able to feel them (the weeds) between my fingers,' I used to say, and my non-glove-wearing friends still do say. A kind of mystical religious fervour enters the voice as the words are uttered. Well, I can tell you all, now, that that's just my eye. It's easy to weed in gloves and it's no less efficient. And it's marvellous, incidentally, how clean your hands keep. The one disadvantage is that the handles of whatever tools you're using do tend to get plastered with mud and that this isn't automatically rubbed off.

Weeding on your hands and knees means that your eyes are close to the ground – the scene of operations. They should always travel just ahead of the trowel point so that the unusual can be observed before it is destroyed. I never like to weed out anything that I can't identify. Not all seedlings are weeds. You may feel that life is too short to leave a seedling in till it's large enough to identify. My own feeling is that life's too interesting not to leave it there until you can identify it. Taking this view, you will very soon learn to recognize weed seedlings when they are no larger than a pair of seed leaves. The not so easily identified ones will then most probably turn out to be the progeny of some of your border plants or shrubs, and it may suit you to save and grow them on.

For instance, the elegant and feathery mauve *Thalictrum delavayi*, revelling in a nice wet soil like ours, is a herbaceous plant that never needs disturbing and does not readily lend itself to division anyway. But in early summer you will nearly always find its seedlings in the neighbourhood of old plants. They can be pricked out into a seed box and, later on, lined out, and they may even, given individual treatment, carry a few blooms in their first autumn. *Mertensia virginica* is another plant with the welcome habit of self-sowing. The seed leaves are shaped like Spades in playing-cards, and are glaucous. Here again, if the seedlings are pricked out, they will develop very quickly and continue to grow long after the parent plants have died off for the season. Next spring they will be full of flowers themselves. *Dicentra spectabilis*, the Bleeding Heart, is none too easy a plant to multiply by vegetative methods, but it usually sets seeds and in some years the babies come up quite thickly around their parents. They look rather like fumitory seedlings, to which they are closely related.

Seedlings can be very deceptive. None more so than the various brands of what I loosely term the lesser willowherbs. They are the small-flowered, tall-growing species and natural hybrids of *Epilobium*: a thoroughly promiscuous crowd, and insidious, too. They have often managed to flower and seed before you have become aware of their presence, and they are abominably prolific. In winter they make a dense basal rosette and you may be almost certain that any gardener you employ will fail to weed them, or any other rosette-forming plant, out. They look precious. Quite often, they look remarkably like small sweet william plants.

When weeds are growing fast and healthily, they are always easier to extract than on a piece of ground where they have been allowed to form a dense mat and are in a half starved condition. So, generous feeding of the garden is a good plan, even if it does benefit weed growth. When visitors exclaim 'What a year it is for weeds!' (which they do, every year), I'm apt to point out that if the weeds won't grow, nothing else will. Weeds that are growing healthily will not run to seed nearly as quickly as those that are starved and this gives you more breathing space in which to get around to coping with them.

Eleanor Perényi
Green Thoughts, 1981

Sooner or later every gardener must face the fact that certain things are going to die on him. It is a temptation to be anthropomorphic about plants, to suspect that they do it to annoy. One knows, after all, that they lead lives of their own: plant the lily bulb in the center of the bed and watch it come up under a brick near the edge; pull up a sick little bush and throw it on the compost heap, and ten to one, it will obstinately revive. Usually, though, gardening failures, like airplane crashes, are the result of 'human error,' of not reading the directions or paying attention.

It may be something as simple as absent-mindedly liming the hydrangea, or as subtle as not noticing that a streetlight shines all night on the chrysanthemum bed – chrysanthemum bloom is triggered by long dark nights and a persistent light may confuse them. A dog may regularly visit a bush that is turning yellow. The gardener must keep his eye peeled, as much for the things that do well as those that do badly. The two are related. The acid soil that favors the iris is bad for the peonies, and trying to grow them together doesn't work. You could learn this from a book but also from simple observation. People who blame their failures on 'not having a green thumb' (and they are legion) usually haven't done their homework. There is of course no such thing as a green thumb. Gardening is a vocation like any other – a calling, if you like, but not a gift from heaven. One acquires the necessary skills and knowledge to do it successfully, or one doesn't. The ancients gardened without guidance from books, by eye and by hand, and while I am a devotee of gardening books and love to study and quarrel with them, I don't think they are a substitute for practical experience, any more than cookbooks are.

One must, to begin with, acquire a mental map of the terrain, know where falls the shadow, where shines the sun – and when. For several seasons I made the elementary mistake of planting shrub roses in early spring, in locations that were full of sun at that time. Three months later, I would discover that the July sun vanished behind the street elms by two in the afternoon, and that the roses did poorly as a result. One learns these things eventually, but it takes time, which is why the gardener should hold his hand for at least a year before making any permanent arrangements. Until a twelve-month cycle has revolved, he won't know where are the low spots that collect moisture and freeze hard in winter, where the dessicating west wind does its evil work, or the opposite: where is the cosy corner in which the tender seedlings can most safely be trusted to winter over?

There is no substitute for observation, and it must be never-ending. Overnight, the enemy leaves his campfires burning and steals a march. The hedge looks all right, doesn't it? Pass a hand over the surface and a cloud of – what, white fly? – ascends. Perhaps a shower of reddened needles falls to earth. The hedge is *not* all right; you might have noticed this weeks ago and, if like me you don't care to spray, done the organic and just as effective thing and turned a blast of water from the hose on it. Predators of all kinds move with supernatural speed in summer. One day the tomato vines are the picture of health. Go away for the weekend, and when you return they look as though rats had been at them. It isn't rats, it's the tomato worm who wears so wonderful a green-and-black camouflage that you may stare at the plant for half an hour without seeing him. (When you do, fetch the scissors and cut him in half, a disgusting business but much safer than spraying.) Other troubles may be more insidious, take longer to diagnose. Often, for instance, we don't realize the effect of a tree on its surroundings – how much water it absorbs, how far the roots extend – and are correspondingly disappointed when ground covers or other plants fail to survive even at what seems a safe distance.

Nevertheless, not all failures are self-imposed, the result of ignorance, carelessness or inexperience. It takes a while to grasp that a garden isn't a testing ground for character and to stop asking, what did I do wrong? Maybe nothing. Some plantsmen abet guilt feelings – and incidentally try to protect themselves – with warnings that their product has been inspected and mailed to you in perfect condition. The rest, they imply, is up to you. No matter that it arrives looking like a wad of wet moss, no way to tell which end is up, or a dried-up stick in a bag: if nothing comes of it, the fault is yours. Not so. There is a great deal wrong with the way many plants are grown and shipped today. Half-a-dozen years ago, the nurseries in my neighborhood grew their own stock and were responsible for it. Mail-order houses were equally scrupulous, and the best still are. But more and more the average garden center is relying on mass production for its overgrown annuals, unpinched and about to bloom; perennials that might have been baked in clay; and those shrubs whose burlapped roots look and feel like cannonballs. Of course you are a fool to buy these, and in that sense the resulting failure is on your own head. But there may be nothing else readily to hand, and a dozen reasons why there is no time to scour the catalogues and wait for weeks for plants that may be no better than the garden-center ones when they do arrive. Seed, too, is unreliable in spite of vacuum packs and dating, and if it is properly sown and tended and does not germinate or produce healthy plants, it is occasion not for hand-wringing and self-reproach but for an angry letter to the source. I love Beverley Nichols for having the same trouble I do. But it could also be that his alstromerias were a bad lot.

Tyler Whittle
Some Ancient Gentlemen, 1965

That a layman should find the zeal of a botanist absurd is barely surprising, but the orthodox gardener often shares his opinion. He is bewildered by such a strange enthusiasm for *wild* plants. There are plants enough on the market as it is. Too many. Everyone's choice is spoilt by the increasing number and thickness of commercial catalogues. Secretly he believes his collecting colleagues are mildly dotty; that to enlarge the flora still further is a waste of effort. But then he begins to understand part of the compulsion when, in someone else's garden, he is confronted by a beautiful flower which he has never seen before and which he immediately wants for himself.

English gardeners in particular, unless they are tightly self-controlled, give way very easily to the temptation to acquire anything beautiful and new. We are all floral magpies because we want to possess beauty, though in plant life, as in everything else from primitive cave paintings to handsome machine-tooled engines, there is no orthodox and rigid canon of beauty. One gardener will rave about the drooping luxuriance of the Amaranthus, Prince's Feather, while his neighbour is just as besotted by a wild Fig Marigold from the Scilly Isles. Standards are personal and vary considerably, but botanists mostly share a liking for elegant simplicity in flowers, and this makes the whole world their garden. Hunting for beauty is the primary impulse which can drive them to such excesses.

Another obvious impulse is the attraction of rarity. If a plant is beautiful as well, so much the better; but its uncommonness is sufficient reward. The same force which excites the Hatton Garden experts whenever they handle an unusual precious stone drives botanists out of doors in search of rarities. They do not expect a great deal. There are few botanical Everests to conquer and

nothing in the science compares to the splitting of the atom, but they have the same adventurousness as mountaineers and the same methodical approach as a trained physicist. The strict scientists among them assemble their data from every possible source and permit themselves an amount of intelligent conjecture. They are gratified by finding a rarity because it is a scientific accomplishment. The other collectors are equally gratified, but for a less detached reason. Put simply, this is the emotional pleasure of being the first, or amongst the first few, to know, see, or do anything at all. And for this – the hope of finding an unrecorded species, or even aberrant shoots, peculiar cross-breeds, infertile mutes, and vegetable mulattoes, quadroons, and octoroons, botanists will put up with discomfort, fatigue, indignity, and danger. Though, it is not, of course, always necessary.

Katharine S. White
Onward and Upward in the Garden, 1979

By August a flower garden, at least on the coast of eastern Maine, where I live, can be at its best – and at its worst. Most of one's successes are apparent, and all of one's failures. For me, this year, heavy memories remain from spring of the disaster area in the north bed of old-fashioned roses, where field mice, hungry under a snowdrift, stripped the bark off the bushes and killed two-thirds of them. Like all disaster areas, this one is still, although replanted, rather bleak. A more recent sorrow is the sudden death on the terrace of a well-established Jackmani clematis, which turned black over-night just as its big purple blossoms were opening. There are numerous theories in the household about this loss – too heavy a dose of fertilizer, too much watering, too strong a spray drifting over from the nearby rose beds, a disease still undiagnosed. My own theory is dachshund trouble. Our dachshund is a robin-and-bee hound, not a badger hound. A robust dog, he flings himself with abandon at birds, bees, and fireflies. Once he caught a barn swallow on the wing. Bees swarm all over the clematis bed, attracted by the petunias and violas, the foxgloves and lilies that we grow in front of the clematis, to give the vines the recommended 'cool root run.' I think the dachshund mortally wounded the Jackmani vine in a scuffle with a bee, for the other large-flowered clematis vines in that bed are spreading their mauve and mulberry stars all over the cedar windbreak, and the roses are in their second surge of bloom. The terrace, despite its accident, is one of our successes, and so, it would seem, are the long borders of perennials, with their masses of hardy phlox, which, because it is mid-August, are in full color. Yet a closer look at the borders will show that even here all is not well. The wars of aggression that I thought our private Security Council and its little army of two, armed with spade, fork, and trowel, had settled in early spring have started again. The lolloping day lilies have begun to blot out the delicate columbines, the clumps of feathery white achilleas are strangling the far more precious delphiniums, and the phlox itself is at the throats of the lupines and the Canterbury bells. Even the low plants at the front of the borders are making aggressive sorties. The ajuga, whose small blue spires were so beautiful in June and early July, is one of the worst offenders. Unless I soon repress its insinuating roots, there will be no violets, pansies, or pinks next year. (I should have known better than to plant the stuff in the first place; after all, the ajuga's familiar name, bugleweed, carries its own warning.) There is also internecine warfare among the phlox – between the burgeoning clumps of common pink, white, and calico phlox and the less well-established stands of the newer varieties, whose colors are more interesting. Nonetheless, I am happy with all this bountiful bloom, and, careless gardener that I am, I comfort myself with the thought that at least I have achieved a mass effect, and that the flowers grow in drifts of color in a way that even Gertrude Jekyll, the author of *Colour in the Flower Garden*, might have approved. But that formidable garden genius of the last generation would never, never have condoned my crowded beds or my state of August sloth, which makes me want to say, 'Oh, let it go. Let the plants fight their own battles.'

It is in moods like this that a garden of flowering shrubs seems wonderfully easy and peaceful. Shrubs grow slowly. They need less care, less

adjudication, less ruthless cutting back than perennials. We have never grown many shrubs here, probably because a well-landscaped shrubbery does not seem to suit our rural countryside. We do have a few, but they are the common ones, seen on almost every farm – lilacs, spiraea, honeysuckle bush, and shrub roses. Yet flowering shrubs are dear to me. I grew up in a house where the beauty of the shrubbery far surpassed that of the flower beds. We actually lived on a Hawthorn Road, in a suburb of Boston, and the street was named for the three huge English hawthorn trees that grew in our own yard – a red, a pink, and a white. Towering above the lilacs in the curving bed of shrubs, they were a sight to see in May. Only the most ambitious nursery catalogues seem to list hawthorn any more, and when they do they are apt to spell it 'hawthorne,' such is the carrying power of Nathaniel. To reach our May blossoms, we children had to carry a stepladder into the empty lot next door, use it for the first boost up, and then scramble the rest of the way to a narrow ledge on top of an enormously high lattice fence that backed our shrubbery. Standing there perilously, trying to keep our balance, we had to reach *up* to break the branches. Memory makes the fence at least twenty feet high, and the hawthorn trees many feet higher, but remembered Boston snowdrifts still tower way over my head, so perhaps our hawthorns were only the average height of eighteen or twenty feet. At that, they were the tallest of the shrubs.

Most people do not pick their flowering shrubs, but we always did. I can remember the succession of flowering branches, plucked by the adults of the household and arranged by them in a tall gray Chinese jar, in our gold-and-green parlor. My sister and I and our friends had a game we played with the shrubbery. It was called Millinery. All the little girls in the neighborhood would bring to our lawn their broad-brimmed straw school hats, which, because they were Boston girls' hats, had only plain ribbon bands for decoration. Then each of us would trim her straw with blossoms from the shrubs. There was a wide choice of trimmings – forsythia, Japanese crab, Japanese quince, mock orange, flowering almond, lilac, hawthorn, bridal wreath, weigela, deutzia, with its tiny white bells, and, in June, altheas and shrub roses. We were not allowed to pick the rhododendrons or the azaleas, but nothing else was forbidden. When our flowery concoctions were completed, we put them on our heads and proudly paraded into the house to show them off to our elders; it seems to me now that we must have made quite a gay sight. By dusk the trimmings were dead, and the next day we could start all over again.

Russell Page
The Education of a Gardener, 1962

I know that I cannot make anything new. To make a garden is to organise all the elements present and add fresh ones, but first of all, I must absorb as best I can all that I see, the sky and the skyline, the soil, the colour of the grass and the shape and nature of the trees. Each half-mile of countryside has its own nature and every few yards is a reinterpretation. Each stone where it lies says something of the earth's underlying structure; and the plants growing there, whether native or exotic, will indicate the vegetable chemistry of that one place.

Such things show the limitations of a site and limitations imply possibilities. A problem is a challenge. I cannot remember a completely characterless site though, for example, a walled rectangle of sandy earth in the Nile Valley with not a tree visible would seem to qualify as such. So would a stretch of flat sugar-beet field in the industrial North of France with pylons of high tension wires standing across a bleak landscape relieved only by factory chimneys on the horizon. Even so you can always turn to something for a starting point. In the first (an actual case) the hot blue sky, cloudless all the year round, offered an easy answer – shade. A garden should be devised through which one would always walk in shade. Shade implied trees. A mango grove became the main theme of the garden and all its parts and details were subjected to the over-riding theme. For another reason trees, too, were the answer in the second case: not for shade, but to bring

an illusion of wilder country into a man-spoilt landscape. Time was a factor here. The house was ugly and there was little labour available for the upkeep of a garden. I chose to plant young birch trees, and now, twenty years later, the house is veiled in a haze of birches light enough not to steal the sun, while their branches and the haphazard colonnade of their silvered trunks hide the ugly view.

Unlike painting or sculpture or buildings a garden grows. Its appearance changes – plants mature, some in six weeks, some in six hundred years. There are few gardens that can be left alone. A few years of neglect and only the skeleton of a garden can be traced – the modelling of the ground perhaps, walls or steps, a pool, the massing of trees. Japanese artists working with a few stones and sand four hundred years ago achieved strangely lasting compositions. However there, too, but for the hands that have piously raked the white sand into patterns and controlled the spread of moss and lichens, little would remain.

We live under an accumulation of periods and styles and cultures. The variations of artistic expression over the whole world for the last four thousand years are available, a vast store of information making a vast confusion. Architecture has found a way out through functionalism and has largely become applied and often splendid engineering. Painters and sculptors, struggling to free themselves from a top-heavy load, have experimented with association-patterns dug from the different layers of their consciousness.

I think that creative gardening need not suffer from these, the results of a changing, if not a disintegrating culture. It can begin from another point. A seed, a plant, a tree must each obey the laws of its nature. Any serious interference with these and it must die. It will only grow and thrive when the conditions for it are approximately right. If you wish to make anything grow you must understand it, and understand it in a very real sense. 'Green fingers' are a fact, and a mystery only to the unpractised. But green fingers are the extensions of a verdant heart. A good garden cannot be made by somebody who has not developed the capacity to know and to love growing things.

Michael Pollan
Second Nature, 1991

I am alleged to have one, at least by those of my friends who garden with less success than I do. That's usually how it goes with a green thumb – nobody quite believes it of themselves, but when you find someone whose beefsteaks are fat and red by July, and whose delphiniums soar like periwinkle skyscrapers over the prosperous city of their perennial border, the term fairly leaps to the tongue. It figures: Your own failures will seem more bearable if the other gardener has a gift from the gods.

Though I am reasonably sure there is such a thing, I'm not about to number myself among the graced and elect. It would be, I don't know, a bit presumptuous. Maybe even dangerous – like I was really asking for it. (How about a blast of August frost, Mister Green Thumb? Or maybe a plague of aphids?) I guess I'm a little like the Calvinist who doesn't dare assume anything about his status, gracewise. And even though he knows it's probably already settled, he's either got it or he doesn't, he's going to keep working at it anyway, just to be on the safe side, cover all the bases. Besides, by now my alleged green thumb (Let *them* say it!) is a reputation I feel obliged to at least try to uphold. So I fret over my transplants, monitor my soil closely, thumb through the reference books – as if good works in the garden might be taken for grace. All of which makes my many failures that much harder to bear.

Consider my carrots. Every spring I planted them, and every summer I pulled from my soil this very sorry collection of gnarled, arthritic digits – all knuckle, and not one more than two inches long. I might have learned to accept this gap in my gardening repertoire except for the fact that carrots are generally regarded as one of the easier vegetables to grow. They come up readily from seed, few pests have a taste for them, and they're untroubled by frost. Buy one of those 'child's first garden' kits and it's bound to contain a packet of carrot seeds. That's not only because carrots figure prominently in the childhood imagination (think of Bugs Bunny, Captain Kangaroo), but because they're considered more or less 'foolproof.'

What sort of green thumb could I possibly have if I couldn't grow a carrot? This failure was an embarrassment, frankly, and a crisis of my gardening faith.

So I determined to get it right, to know carrots. I thought long and hard about them. I even tried to think what my carrots might be thinking – to imagine what it was about their situation they didn't like. Their tops were lush and green, so their complaint was not about the food or water. Could it be the company? One year they occupied a plot next to the onions, a dubious neighborhood for any plant. (Onions are as controversial in the society of plants as in our own; many species recoil from them.) So the next season I relocated them to a spot by a row of comparatively genial lettuces – and observed no improvement.

What does a carrot care about? This is not as dumb a question as it sounds. It is more than an anthropomorphic conceit to attribute likes and dislikes to plants, to wonder, if not about how they're 'feeling,' then at least about what matters to them, what they require in order to fulfill the terms of their destiny. Most of the good gardeners I've met seem to possess a faculty, akin to empathy, that allows them to sense what their plants might need at any time. 'If you wish to make anything grow,' Russell Page wrote in *The Education of a Gardener*, 'you must understand

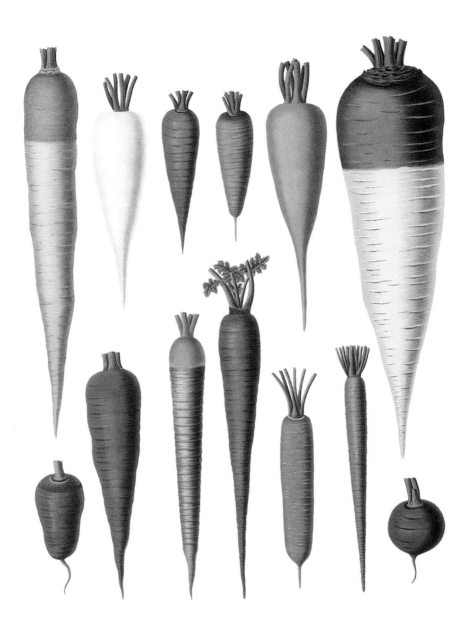

it, and understand it in a very real sense. "Green fingers" are a fact, and a mystery only to the unpractised. But green fingers are the extensions of a verdant heart.' I don't think Page is merely being sentimental here. He's speaking of the need in gardening for an imaginative leap – in my case, into the innermost nature of carrothood. And this is what I attempted. I considered, What would matter most to a carrot as it struggled to get past the pinkie stage? And it came to me: shoulder room.

I pictured a cross section of the first few inches of my soil and it was a Number 6 train at rush hour, jammed with cramped orange commuters. My carrots stood too close together; I had been insufficiently ruthless when it came to thinning the seedlings. (This seems to be a common failing among inexperienced gardeners; killing off that which you've just planted seems wasteful, even cruel, but triage is essential in the case of root crops.) And I imagined something else, too: that a carrot, aspiring to drive its taproot straight down into the earth, would want an airy soil, no hard clumps or stones to impede its thrust. Had I given my carrots such a root run? It was easy to find out. I stuck my index finger into the soil and barely reached the second knuckle before jamming up against thick, wet clay. My soil was too heavy for carrots.

Success, they say, is a matter of being in the right place at the right time. Perhaps more than is the case in life, in the garden you can often alter the place (and indeed sometimes even the time). I set about giving my carrots a more propitious place by lightening the soil in which they grew. As early in the spring as the ground could be worked, I dug in a bag of builder's sand, a bale of peat moss, and as much compost as I could spare. Ordinarily, carrots wouldn't warrant such a heavy investment of compost, but much was at stake, and nothing works better to lighten a clay soil. I mixed everything together by hand, taking care to remove stones and crush clay clumps as I went along. It took only a few moments of kneading before the consistency of the soil, formerly as dense as fudge, lightened to that of cake. I stuck my finger in again, and sunk without effort to the depth of a cigar. Here was carrot utopia.

After raking the area level and smooth, I sowed two rows of Mokum, a reputedly extra-sweet snub-nosed carrot from France. In a week there emerged a feathery strip of seedlings which I scrupulously thinned to an interval of one inch; a month after, I thinned it again to make absolutely sure my carrots would never have to jostle one another. Everybody now had a seat, and by August I was pulling out of the ground long, orange panatelas, some of the handsomest carrots, I don't mind saying, that I had ever seen. Harvesting root crops has to be one of gardening's finer pleasures. There's the element of surprise (until now, you could only infer by foliage what might be going on down there), and, even better, the small miracle of finding form and color and value amid the earth's black and undifferentiated mass. It's gold prospecting writ small, and these carrots represented quite a strike. I wiped one clean on my shirt, buffed it bright, and then tasted its cool, subterranean sweetness, its unexpectedly intense . . . carrotness.

Maybe, I thought to myself, maybe I did have a green thumb.

Margery Fish
A Flower for Every Day, 1965

June is the month that takes care of itself. Even the dullest garden can't help being colourful in June. When the cow parsley reaches shoulder level in the hedgerows and the roadside is scented with honeysuckle and wild roses the garden too seems to grow up overnight. This is the time when one discovers if one has planted too closely, and I always have, and if one has staked sufficiently and efficiently, and I never have.

June is the month when roses tumble over the walls, the tall spikes of delphiniums tower above the jungle of the borders, at the mercy of the gales that nearly always turn up some time in June, to humble our pride and challenge our foresight. The farmers take the 'June drop' in their stride. Though it flattens the corn and brings violent rain to devastate the hay, it also thins out the apples for them. The poor gardener has no such compensations for his shattered hopes.

I have some really lovely white Pacific delphiniums and when we have a wet May they outdo themselves in height. The taller they get the more brittle are their hollow stems and nothing can save them if we have a good rousing gale. I know if I had time to give each tall spike an individual cane they would be safe, but that I'll never be able to do. Peasticks might work if I could ever get them in sufficiently deep, which I know I can't unless my heavy clay soil changes its form overnight. My iron halfhoop supports are magnificent for most occasions, but they are too unresisting for tall

delphiniums and other hollow-stemmed perennials, and in a bad blow the fragile stems are broken or crushed against the iron.

I wish there was some way to keep delphiniums within reasonable proportions. Michaelmas daisies, heleniums and golden-rod can be cut down when they have reached about 12 inches and they will grow again, but only to half their normal height. I am afraid it wouldn't work with delphiniums because the stems of the second lot of flowers are often nearly as tall as the first ones. Nothing will stop plant breeders producing bigger flowers on taller stems, and all we can hope for is that there is some way of producing stronger stems to carry the weight of blooms.

William Bowyer Honey
Gardening Heresies and Devotions, 1939

In those spacious Victorian times which were the heyday of William Robinson and his fellow apostles every big 'place' in the fashion had its wild garden, often of great extent, maintained often at great cost. Nowadays they are fewer, but every estate with land not actually given over to farming or garden cultivation may be in a sense a wild garden, though it is not easy (and perhaps not desirable) to draw a dividing line. The wild garden merges on the one hand into the garden proper; on the other it may easily lapse into mere neglected ground, and it is certain that many well-intended wild gardens are rightly regarded by farmers as breeding grounds for noxious weeds. This points to the essence of the whole matter. A wild garden is a place where one grows weeds of one's own choice, by constant trial and failure finding the soil and situation in which they can survive in cut-throat competition with all manner of rivals. The process is enormously wasteful, like very much else in nature. Even with the widest knowledge of habitat it is impossible to be sure in advance that everything sown or planted will succeed. Perseverance over many years is called for. It is a common ambition to wish to naturalize in this way attractive foreign plants, and a praiseworthy success with such Southern alpines as *Anemone appennina* and the like should not blind us to the dangers of introducing into our fields the more prolific composites (for example) of other lands, which might well take possession as the Prickly Pear has done in Australia.

Every not-too-well-cared-for meadow is a potential wild garden, and a well-hedged small field or paddock, to be scythed with discrimination perhaps twice in the year, can be an enviable possession if placed where its harvest of seeds will not be blown as a nuisance into cultivated ground. The rampant plants – dock, dandelion, plantain, thistle – can be reduced by spudding and by cutting before they seed, but no right-minded wild-gardener would wish all of even these 'weeds' to be entirely banished. Even the large true dandelion may be admitted in moderation, while the related hawkweeds and hawkbits (all are dandelions to many lawn-keepers) are actually delightful things in themselves, however menacing the sight of their 'clocks' may be to the careful cultivator. The orange-red hawkweed is in fact a more beautiful thing than many border plants, but to know that it is in Canada, under the name of the Devil's Paint-Brush, the most dreaded of noxious weeds is enough to bring home the true character and dangers of the wild garden. In dry ground this hawkweed will flourish, as will the delicate Maiden Pink, the pale blue chicory, and several wild geraniums and Crane's-Bills, to mention only a few of the beautiful wild flowers of the chalk regions of the south of England. The hedges of such a corner of ground give a further opportunity for starting the lovely wild clematis, the poisonous bryony with its amazingly beautiful tendrils, and many other native ramblers if not already there. In moister land a neglected meadow will give even more exciting results. Such treasured wild flowers as the spotted and purple orchis and the Snake's Head fritillary (which is truly wild in England, it is said, only in the Iffley meadows) may perhaps be induced to thrive, and such grand things as the wild Meadow Sweet are almost certain to do so.

But meadows are by no means the only sort of wild garden. A piece of thin woodland, however small, will give endless opportunity. If it is of oak or birch the plants will have a better chance than among the beeches, with their hungry surface-roots. But the spring beauty of the beech, its autumn colour, and the red-brown of its winter carpet, almost compensate for the extra trouble given. It is good to contrive a mossy woodland path, with a succession of incidents from early spring almost to midsummer. Blue anemones, hepaticas, *Scilla sibirica* and the *Chionodoxas, Muscari*, daffodils, and the various sorts of wild hyacinth, all of them common things, will provide a pageant unsurpassable by any 'novelties'. If they are boldly and freely grouped, with due intervals, they can have no better setting than the carpet of leaves and moss and the slender woodland grasses. On the margins of such woodland, snowdrops, aconites and primroses should flourish; in the half shade, tall mulleins, foxgloves and willow-herb will find their *optimum* conditions; at the foot of the trees exquisite cyclamens of several almost indistinguishable kinds will make little colonies, and in the more deeply shaded corners the glossy-leaved barberries and periwinkles will grow vigorously, and need only the encouragement of a very little sunshine to flower freely. In such a place no more control is needed than to check the spread of bramble and bracken; both can be beautiful, but they will on occasion overstep the limits of even that wide toleration which should be the first principle of wild gardening.

Such places have lessons to teach the maker of more strictly cultivated gardens, especially if garden design is thought of as primarily the use, with a wide taste and knowledge, of the happy accidents of Nature. The wood edge, with its line broken into bays and promontories, now reaching out overhead, now gathered in compact masses, is a model for the designer of

borders; natural spacing
may show within the
wood, here a dense holly bush,
there a towering tree, and near them,
composing a perfect natural group,
a loose clump of alder or field-maple
with a drift of blue-bells breaking away
from its foot. A woodland
vista is another inspiring
possession, admitting
sidelong shafts of
sunshine and framing
a distant view, while
changing levels, with
ground sweeping easily
or abruptly to secluded
hollows, and above all the
sense of a third dimension given by growth
overhead, can fruitfully suggest much excellent
garden design, on however small a scale. Some
things there must be of course which are peculiar to the woods and
beyond imitation: as to see, through an opening in the tops of the tall
shadowy trees among which one stands, the tops of other and taller trees
rising blue and gold in misty morning sunshine and among them birds
wheeling and alighting.

Vita Sackville-West
In Your Garden Again, 1953

A friend of mine, whose own fingers are of the greenest, reproaches me from time to time for making gardening sound too easy. My optimism, she says, is misleading. Yet I try to avoid recommending 'difficult' plants, or at any rate to accompany them always with a warning. The truth is probably that most plants are temperamental, except the weeds, which all appear to be possessed of magnificent constitutions. The mystery of the Madonna lily, for instance, has never been satisfactorily explained. *Daphne mezereum* provides another puzzle: you may observe all the rules, but nothing will make her flourish if she does not intend to do so. Then there is the case of the self-sown seedling, which, sprouting up in apparently impossible conditions, excels in health and vigour anything similar which you may have transplanted with the greatest care into a prepared bed of the most succulent consistency.

In my own garden I have a curious example of the perverse behaviour of plants. Two cuttings of a poplar, brought home in a sponge-bag from Morocco, were both struck and planted out at the same time. Same age, same parent, same aspect, same soil; yet, fifteen years later, one is only half the size of the other. Why? I can suppose only that like two children of identical begetting and upbringing, they differ in constitution and character.

It thus becomes evident that gardening, unlike mathematics, is not an exact science. It would be dull if it were. Naturally, there are certain laws whose transgression means disaster: you would not plant an azalea in a chalk pit. I do agree with my friend, however, that writers on gardening very often omit to make some elementary comments, pointing out possible causes of failure. This brings me to two things I wanted to say. The first is about snowdrops. The time to move them, if you wish to do so, is just after they have flowered; in other words, now. (Do not cut off their heads as they are very generous in seeding themselves.) The second thing is about mice. They eat bulbs, leaving large bare patches where one has planted snowdrops and crocuses. I asked an eminent nurseryman what one could do about this, and he replied that as one soaked peas in red lead before sowing them, he could see no reason why the same procedure should harm bulbs. It would be an experiment worth trying, because there is no doubt that distressing gaps do appear, for which I can find no explanation except mice. Besides, there are tell-tale little holes.

I am ashamed of having forgotten to mention the blue anemone hepatica as occupants of a winter corner, last week. They should on no account be omitted.

The more I see of other people's gardens the more convinced do I become of the value of good grouping and shapely training. These remarks must necessarily apply most forcibly to gardens of a certain size, where sufficient space is available for large clumps or for large specimens of individual plants, but even in a small garden the spotty effect can be avoided by massing instead of dotting plants here and there.

It is a truly satisfactory thing to see a garden well schemed and wisely planted. Well schemed are the operative words. Every garden, large or small, ought to be planned from the outset, getting its bones, its skeleton, into the shape that it will preserve all through the year even after the flowers have

faded and died away. Then, when all colour has gone, is the moment to revise, to make notes for additions, and even to take the mattock for removals. This is gardening on the large scale, not in details. There can be no rules, in so fluid and personal a pursuit, but it is safe to say that a sense of substance and solidity can be achieved only by the presence of an occasional mass breaking the more airy companies of the little flowers.

What this mass shall consist of must depend upon many things: upon the soil, the aspect, the colour of neighbouring plants, and above all upon the taste of the owner. I can imagine, for example, a border arranged entirely in purple and mauve – phlox, stocks, pansies, clematis Jackmanii trained over low hoops – all planted in bays between great promontories of the plum-coloured sumach, *Rhus cotinus foliis purpureis*, but many people, thinking this too mournful, might prefer a scheme in red and gold. It would be equally easy of accomplishment, with a planting of the feathery *Thalictrum glaucum, gallardias, Achillea eupatorium* (the flat-headed yellow yarrow), *helenium, Lychnis chalcedonica*, and a host of other ordinary, willing, herbaceous things. In this case, I suppose, the mass would have to be provided by bushes of something like the golden privet or the golden yew, both of which I detest when planted as 'specimens' on a lawn, but which in so aureate a border would come into their own.

The possibilities of variation are manifold, but on the main point one must remain adamant; the alternation between colour and solidity, decoration and architecture, frivolity and seriousness. Every good garden, large or small, must have some architectural quality about it; and, apart from the all-important question of the general lay-out, including hedges, the best way to achieve this imperative effect is by massive lumps of planting such as I have suggested.

I wish only that I could practise in my own garden the principles which I so complacently preach, week after week, in this column.

Henry Mitchell
The Essential Earthman, 1981

Toads are conservative animals, I think, and not much given to expecting the best from fortune. Some weeks ago, well before the end of October, I accidentally dug one up while turning over some garden earth. I was surprised, naturally, when one of the clods heaved over on its side and there, in some annoyance, sat a toad.

These are more expressive animals than the average mammal thinks, and it is not just my imagination, surely, that makes me recognize emotions in them. Often in the spring I have seen them ecstatic – it must be something about the eyes – but more often I have seen them disgruntled and resigned to the absurdity of daily life. They look especially baleful when the gardener accidentally digs them up after they have begun their long cold-weather period of inactivity. They also register disapproval when a hound, or indeed any other dog, picks them up in his mouth. On several occasions I have seen dogs do this, and on all occasions the toad looked angry rather than afraid.

As most gardeners know, it is only young dogs that pick up toads, and they usually do it only once, though Luke, who as the vet correctly said was always going to be 'a very slow dog,' tried toads twice. I have never heard of even young dogs harming the toad nor, for that matter, carrying it in his mouth more than a few feet. Toads, I have been told, secrete a bitter or acrid substance which the dog does not like. Usually once is enough, and toads are left alone after that.

It seems to me odd that I have rarely seen a dead toad, although I know they are mortal. Do they die in ponds, or perhaps under a pile of brushwood?

There are many sorts of toads, and once years ago I went so far as to order an assortment of several kinds from a dealer in Topeka, Kansas, whose name and address I have lost. The different kinds (except tree toads) strike me as rather much alike.

We have all read that each toad eats something like four trillion bugs a week, and that the toad is therefore good to have in the garden. I found that in my part of the city there was a shortage of toads; in fact I never saw any and my neighbors said there were none. Fortunately, I was able to find some tadpoles (toad tadpoles are easily recognized, since they alone are jet black) in a shallow rock pool along the canal at Great Falls last spring, and these grew nicely for a few weeks in the lily pool, then developed legs and hopped out. For some time I saw no young toads, but recently I have seen a dozen or so, about the size of ping pong balls. They have been very interested in going down some back steps into the basement. My Assistant often finds them hiding behind the washing machine, and I have pointed out the importance of checking that engine before starting it up. It does not seem, on the face of it, there is enough in the basement for a toad to eat, so I steadily remove them to the garden. I release them in a woodpile and trust they go on from there.

It is often said they eat slugs. I have kept my eye out to see this, without ever seeing it happen. It is true, however, that this year we had no five- or six-inch slugs (which we always had before) and for the first time I did not find slugs all over the walk leading to the alley.

The gardener should be more than cautious about spraying bugs, since poisoned bugs cannot be good for toads.

Ladybugs are also fine in the garden; they eat aphids. I never spray the aphids, knowing the ladybugs will soon come. If there are not enough aphids, there will not be any ladybugs, it's as simple as that.

Ladybugs have a terrible habit of getting into wet paint, in my observation, and I have no idea how to get it off them. A paper towel suffices for them to get their feet clean enough to get going, but I fear the chemicals of the paint on their shell cases may kill them.

Like many gardeners I am afraid of wasps and hornets and bumblebees, but honeybees do not alarm me. All these creatures commonly fall into fish pools. Some floats of wood are good for them to latch on to. Often a stick or a tuft from some plant can be extended to them to fish them out. It is astonishing how many bees, which seem dead in the water, will revive if fished out and set on the ground to dry. I do not say the gardener should keep watch night and day for waterlogged bugs, but if one is admiring the fish or the water lilies anyway, it is no extra effort to save a bee or a wasp.

I am not sure how we got going on garden animals, but since we're at it, the Carolina box turtle has not been seen for several weeks. He has lived in the neighborhood for several years, wandering from yard to yard. He thinks especially well of my neighbor's woodpile. Last year he hibernated in the ground (late October) in front of the house beneath a kerria bush. I did not think he was burrowing down far enough, but thought it presumptuous to do his digging for him, and apparently he knew what he was about since he emerged in April and has been healthy all summer. Box turtles are too often victims of cars going down alleys. I would never introduce a tortoise of any kind to a garden unless its security could be guaranteed. If one is already there, supplemental feedings of melon rinds are good in the summer. These of course have to be collected after the tortoise has scraped them clean.

Beth Chatto

Dear Friend and Gardener, 1998

Bah! I am perished with cold, my spine chilled to the marrow, after standing out in the equinoctial gale which has been raging through the garden now for more than two days. Out of the East of course. Yet two days ago Andrew and I sat having tea on the lower steps by the house, facing the ponds, basking in low, mellow sunshine, purring at the peaceful scene, backed with tall feathery swamp cypresses, arching bamboos and huge scallop-leaves of gunnera. Around the water's edge, these three are dominant among a hundred other shades and textures of green, so vivid now in the autumn light, with waterlily pads pretending to be cake doyleys, laid out on a dark polished table.

Today the scene is wild, so much tossed and tumbled, the lawns littered with oak twigs and leaves, even small branches, while the leaves of *Betula jacquemontii* speckle the grass with green confetti. Yet, tomorrow may well break calm and innocent as it did in our fruit-farming days, when we woke to find the ground beneath the trees carpeted with apples we had planned all year to harvest. But Andrew taught me to look up and see the major part was still left on the tree. Usually, the smaller apples were whipped off the ends of the branches. Like blood, comparatively few apples spilt look like a lot.

Until the frosts come, whatever the weather, the pot gardens continue to brim over with colour and shapes, probably because they are in sheltered situations, and cosseted almost daily. How can I share them with you without boring you with a long list of names? Perhaps try to give an overall impression?

Looking from the house, or sitting on the south-facing paved area, the view makes me think of a stage set, furnished all the year round, but changing with each season. The lower garden, sloping away, provides a backdrop at this time of year of dark oak and silvery willow. Close to, shrub planting creates a Mediterranean scene, with dry, drought-tolerant plants, many grey-leaved and aromatic. By now, any star performers in this part of the garden have vanished into the wings, but the stage is still beautiful to watch each day as warm autumn sun spotlights the huge tree heather, *Erica arborea*, crowded now with acid-green, flame-shaped young shoots. A strategically placed pot of the grey-leaved *Agave americana* strengthens the planting and repeats in a lighter shade of grey the structure of a large *Yucca gloriosa* planted at the top of a shallow flight of steps. Strong shapes such as these, sometimes a tree or splendid grass, often take the place of sculpture or architecture in my garden.

Feeling enclosed and protected we sit at the table under the magnolia tree and enjoy, to our right, a colourful crowd scene of brimming pots, bowing and smiling cheerfully at us in the sunshine. Pelargoniums in coral-red and salmon shades jostle with the lemon-yellow daisy, *Argyranthemum* 'Jamaica Primrose', all woven through with *Helichrysum petiolare*, both the grey- and yellow-leaved forms. To prevent too many flowering plants looking like an ice-cream soda, I use bold foliage plants set among them, to make strong accents. A large cordyline crowns the group while a phormium with green-and-white striped leaves echoes a particularly handsome pelargonium whose green leaves have broad cream edges. Dark accents are introduced

through the chocolate-coloured rosettes of the tree-like *Aeonium* 'Zwartkop', while low bowls of grey succulents, looking like cool marble, spill onto the paving.

To the left of this large group is another smaller group of pots whose occupants merge into *Romneya coulteri*, still producing huge white poppies, repeating potsful of white-flowered pelargoniums and the white daisy flower, *Argyranthemum frutescens*. Here, the upright branches of the tree poppy are linked to the pots by trailing stems of grey-leaved *Helichrysum petiolare*. Behind them the claret-leaved vine, *Vitis vinifera* 'Purpurea', tumbles from the end of the bedroom wall, repeating the purple-leaved aeonium opposite.

You asked me about the pot gardens outside the little yard over-looked by the utility room window. Several years ago you astonished me by rushing for your camera to take a picture from inside the house of the red cannas and the variegated form of *Arundo donax* soaring up above the window. This year we've done something different. We have made two large groups in the angle formed by the office wall and window, facing south, and the utility room facing east. By this time of the year, it forms such a jungle there is only a tiny path for me to reach the back door. The main eye-catchers are velvety, beetroot-red petunias, rose-pink pelargoniums, an enchanting little lilac-pink nemesia which never stops growing and flowering, and the pink *Argyranthemum* 'Petite Pink'. Again, the froth of colour is relieved by the dark rosettes of aeonium, while jumping out at you are the bold and beautiful leaves of *Plectranthus argentatus*, heavily felted with fine silky hairs. Each morning, I open the door to count the deep blue convolvulus flowers trained round the windows. We've given up trying to grow the super one with the light sky-blue flowers, *Ipomoea tricolor* 'Heavenly Blue' – it sulks too long in early summer if it's the least bit cold.

It's a great relief after the drought to walk now in the Gravel Garden. During August we had, in little offerings, not much more than 15mm (½in) of rain at a time, a total of almost 80mm (3in), very surprising and most welcome. All the plants responded like mad. It is wonderful to see it so colourful, a haze of pink, blue and mauve flowers, interwoven with new foliage which will clothe the area all winter. Ballota and santolina look really handsome now, after being well trimmed in July. *Caryopteris* 'Heavenly Blue' forms large bushes crowded with spires of intense blue flowers, while the second crop of catmint, *Nepeta* 'Six Hills Giant' and the paler *Calamintha nepetoides* (still crowded with bees) make softer washes of colour. An amazing little linaria called 'Antique Silver' has spread several yards along the gravel edge into the hoggin base, looking as if it had the best of conditions. It makes frothy trails of greyish-blue flowers, set off by late blooms of a creamy-yellow poppy, *Eschscholzia californica*, seeded among it. Another invader here is *Clematis orientalis* (*C. tibetana vernayi*), blown in from elsewhere, its sharp, lemon-peel-thick petals and silky seedheads tangling over bergenias and other off-season plants which don't seem to mind the intrusion.

Introducing warm tones among these cool colours are many sedums – wonderful plants, I am so obliged to them, for they are among my most successful tolerators of drought. The well-known *S.* 'Herbstfreude' 'Autumn Joy' is making bold impact, but so too is a newcomer originating from Ewald Hugin, of Freiburg in Germany, called *S.* 'Matrona'. Equally robust, its large heads of rose-pink flowers are intensified by dark green leaves with leaf edges and stems stained purple. Altogether an exciting new plant. Poor soil might be an advantage. If too well fed the large sedums can grow leggy and then fall apart with the weight of their flower-heads.

Edging the curve of one of the island beds is a planting which looks like a patterned shawl dropped onto the pale gravel. *Sedum* 'Bertram Anderson' has clusters of wine-red flowers set against blackish-purple leaves, all weaving through little *Gypsophila repens* 'Rosa Schönheit', still producing sequin-like dots of tiny pink flowers, while the snake-like trails of *Euphorbia myrsinites* form a tassel-like corner.

Euphorbia seguieriana niciciana provides that much-needed touch of acid green – what a long-lasting plant it makes. Throughout the whole length of my dry river-bed garden, *Verbena bonariensis*, seeded in groups here and there, sometimes by the path edge, sometimes in the background, makes graceful screens of purple, both softening and structural, with its bare green strut-like stems carrying clusters of tiny purple flowers for weeks on end. Particularly attractive is where it tangles with the white moth-like flowers of *Gaura lindheimeri* emerging from a patch of the white-flowered *Sedum spectabile* 'Iceberg'.

While writing this I've just realized that almost everything flowering now at the end of September in the Gravel Garden, creating such a welcome summery effect, consists of tiny flowers, held together in dense jewel-like clusters. Grasses wave for attention, but must wait for another letter. I can't bear to rush them.

Anna Pavord
The Tulip, 1999

The small boy, left outside sitting on a rock, had hijacked a passer-by and showed *him* the picture of the flower that I was looking for. 'Omalós,' he said triumphantly as we emerged. 'Omalós,' he said again, pointing at the picture and then somewhere to the west, way over the horizon. The next day I drove myself to Omalós, along narrow roads lined with clouds of blue scabious and heads of wild oats and barley. The backdrop was gargantuan: stony mountain peaks with thick flanks of snow.

Omalós is a bleak town set high on a pancake plain, imprisoned between walls of mountain. The plain was nibbled bare by sheep. It was so quiet that you could hear the seed pods of the wild spurges popping in the heat. I quartered the ground like a blood hound, cheered at finding anemones in all colours, the wild forebears of the florist's 'De Caen'. It seemed likely that where there were anemones, there might also be tulips.

Without realising how much ground I had covered, I found after an hour or so that I was almost halfway up the mountain. The snow-line was clearly visible. I wanted to touch the snow and the track was easy. I calculated that it would take no more than an hour of climbing to get there. When I reached the snow, I found crocus on its melting edges. Even higher were flat, rock-hugging mats of an alpine anchusa, the flowers dazzling blue amongst the leaves. But no tulips.

At the top, I threw a snowball at an eagle before beginning a descent very much more rapid than the upward climb had been. Then, as I mooched back to the car, *Tulipa bakeri* suddenly sprang into view. I thought it was a mirage, but no. While I had been flailing up the 'because-it's-there' route, they had been flowering in an area mercifully fenced off from grazing animals, on the old olive terraces of the Omalós plain. They were growing in thin, poor grassland, their shiny leaves poking out from sheaves of anemones, with orchids thrown in for good measure, as well as the strange pale-green-and-black flowers of *Hermodactylus tuberosus*. I gazed at them in respectful – no, more than that – in reverent silence. I could find nothing suitable to say. This was the first time I had seen tulips growing in the wild. I knew how Galahad must have felt when he finally caught up with the Grail.

At this moment, I happily recognised an obsession that had been creeping up on me for some time. I suppose there must be one or two people in the world who choose not to like tulips, but such an aberration is scarcely credible. Who could resist *T. eichleri* from northern Iran, with its brilliant crimson-scarlet flowers, the petals nipping in slightly at the waist to finish in sharp needle points? The backs of the outer petals are washed over in greeny-buff, so in bud it looks very sober. Then it flings open its petals and reveals itself as the wildly sexy flower that it is. Who could not fall in love with the Cottage tulip 'Magier' as it opens its buds in May? The petals are a soft milky-white splashed with purple around the edges. As the flower ages, which it does gracefully and well (a worthwhile attribute) the whole thing darkens and purple leaches out from the edges through the entire surface of the petals. It is a mesmerising performance.

Edith Wharton
In Morocco, 1920

Court within court, garden beyond garden, reception halls, private apartments, slaves' quarters, sunny prophets' chambers on the roofs and baths in vaulted crypts, the labyrinth of passages and rooms stretches away over several acres of ground. A long court enclosed in pale-green trellis-work, where pigeons plume themselves about a great tank and the dripping tiles glitter with refracted sunlight, leads to the fresh gloom of a cypress garden, or under jasmine tunnels bordered with running water; and these again open on arcaded apartments faced with tiles and stucco-work, where, in a languid twilight, the hours drift by to the ceaseless music of the fountains.

Beverley Nichols
Garden Open Today, 1963

I have a charming elderly neighbour whom we will call Lady D. Her passion for flowers is so intense and her reaction so immediate that her friends live in fear that one day she will see a lily on the other side of the road, forget all about the traffic, and run across to greet it, with fatal consequences. Lady D is often my companion on excursions to the various lovely gardens that are open to the public in our part of the world. And here I must confess that her adoration of flowers occasionally leads her to behave in a manner which might not be approved by the authorities. I can best describe this behaviour by explaining that only too often, when we return home, she triumphantly produces from her bag some blossom which she has purloined when nobody was looking – the bell of a rare fuchsia which she filched from the cool house at . . . never mind where, or a large white camellia which was flowering in the corner of the gardens at X.

When one remonstrates with her about this regrettable tendency she looks at one with an expression of the greatest innocence and protests: 'But my dear, it had *dropped!*' It had, of course, done nothing of the sort. But one does not care to argue with an old lady, so one can only hope for the best, and make a note to keep her under sharper observation on the next excursion.

Well, three summers ago, we went off to visit the gardens at X, which are always almost deserted on weekdays. It was a glorious afternoon, and though it was 'between seasons' there was still a host of giant lilies lighting up the shadows under the oaks. These lilies engaged the attention of Lady D, and she lingered over them for so long that I wandered off to examine something else. When I returned I gave her a searching look. She had left her bag in the car, and she could not possibly have concealed one of those enormous lilies on her person. All seemed to be well until we got home.

And then, she opened her glove and held out her hand.

'What have you been up to this time?'

'It's for you.'

'But what is it?'

'It dropped.'

I made no comment on this outrageous assertion. The stem was still green and had obviously been torn off in a hurry.

'But what *is* it?'

'It's a pod from one of those beautiful white lilies. I thought you might like to plant some of the seeds. When they come up you can give me some.'

'You really must not do these things. One of these days . . .'

She made an impatient gesture. 'I know exactly what you're going to say. One of these days I shall be arrested and sent to prison. Well, if the Tory Government . . .' (Lady D claims to have communist inclinations) 'can't find anything better to do than persecute poor old ladies for picking up flower pods that have dropped . . .'

She caught my eye.

'Or *almost* dropped.'

So the argument ended, as always, in laughter.

And I planted the seeds.

They came up as onions.

At least, that was what we thought they were, when the thin spikes appeared in the following spring.

I said to Page, as we bent over them:'But where on earth did Lady D find onions in the X gardens? And having found them, why should she want to pick them?'

'Beats me. It certainly *looks* like one of onion family.'

'She said she picked it from a lily.'

'Lady D's idea of lilies are a bit vague. Maybe she picked it for a joke?'

'Lady D would never joke about flowers.'

'That's true enough. Anyway, it'll be interesting to see what comes up, when the time comes.'

The time came in August of the following year. We had planted the seedlings in semi-shade, and as the months sped by they grew apace, looking more like onions every day. I was in two minds as to whether they should be pulled up, particularly when the first flower spike appeared, for it was almost indistinguishable from a giant garlic. However, little by little the buds – there were eighteen of them – began to swell, to hang their heads, and to take the shape of bells, until one glorious morning I went out to find that the first of them had fully opened. And it was indeed a snow white bell, like a giant *Leucojum*, six-petalled, with stamens of the palest green. A fortnight later the whole stem was laden with bells which lasted, still glistening, for over six weeks.

When I gathered one of the later flowers, and took it over to Lady D she was like a child to whom one has given some wonderful present. She set it in a slender vase of silver and stared at it in silence. Then she turned to me and said:'And to think that it had dropped, and that I picked it up!'

Anne Scott-James
Gardening Letters to my Daughter, 1990

I have been thinking this weekend about Osbert's contribution to the garden, and really he was a most destructive gardener. True, he sometimes pruned the roses (surprisingly well), and occasionally clipped the box hedges in the front garden (predictably badly), leaving a saddleback depression in the middle of each. He also ruined several beds by introducing rampant plants from his much larger garden at Henley, notably the *Acanthus spinosus* which has swamped various clematis and done in some good nerines.

But he made an enormous contribution in the way of encouragement. He never saw the weeds, only the flowers, and every time we went round the garden he would say 'Darling, I do congratulate you', and mean it.

He also adored our outdoor meals at the slate table, though he carried not so much as a fork from the house, nor took back a single dirty plate. He liked the table properly laid as by a parlour-maid, and at least two courses and Turkish coffee, all of which he got. Goodness, he was spoiled. The coffee, incidentally, I always served in the tiny coffee cups which we bought in a remote mountain village at the end of a terrifying hairpin road in northern Greece, thinking them pleasantly ethnic, only to find when we got home that they were marked 'Made in Japan'.

Karel Čapek
The Gardener's Year, 1929

Gardening man certainly originated by culture and not by natural evolution. If he had originated naturally, he would look different; he would have legs like a beetle so that he would not need to squat, and he would have wings, firstly for their beauty and, secondly, so that he could hover over his borders. Those who have not tried can have no conception of how legs get in a person's way when you have got nothing to stand on; how unnecessarily long they are when you need to fold them under you and poke a finger in the soil; how impossibly short they are when you need to reach the other side of a flowerbed without treading on a pillow of *Pyrethrum* or a budding Columbine. Or to be hung in a sling and dangle over your flora, or at least have four hands and on them a head and a cap and nothing else, or to have telescopic limbs like a photographer's tripod! But since the gardener is outwardly just as maladapted as the rest of you, there is nothing left for him but to show what he can do; to balance on the tip of one foot, to float like an imperial ballerina, to straddle four metres in width, to tread as gently as a butterfly or a wagtail, to get into a square inch of soil, to hold his balance against all laws concerning inclining bodies, to reach everywhere and avoid everything and at the same time try to maintain a certain dignity so that people will not laugh at him.

Of course, at a distant, fleeting glance, you will not see any more of a gardener than his rear end; everything else, like his head, arms and legs, is simply beneath him.

When, in her young days, my late mother used to read her fortune from the cards, she would always whisper over one pile, 'What am I treading on?' At the time, I could not understand why she was so interested in what she was treading on. Only after very many years has it begun to interest me too. I have discovered, to wit, that I am treading on the earth.

We do not really care what we are treading on; we rush somewhere like mad people and at most glimpse what beautiful clouds there are up here or what a beautiful horizon there is back there or what beautiful blue mountains; but we do not look beneath our feet to be able to say and celebrate that the soil is beautiful here. You should have a garden the size of a postage stamp; you should have at least one small flowerbed to learn what you are treading on. Then you would see, dear boy, that not even clouds are as varied, beautiful and dreadful as the soil beneath your feet. You would be able to recognise soil which is acid, viscid, clayey, cold, stony and nasty; you would be able to distinguish topsoil as airy as gingerbread, as warm, light and good as bread, and you would say that it was beautiful, as you now say about women or clouds. You would feel a particular, sensual pleasure as you drove your stick a yard into the crumbly, friable soil or as you crushed a clod in your fist to sample its airy, moist warmth.

And if you cannot appreciate this singular beauty, then may fate bestow a few square yards of clay upon you as a punishment, clay like tin, substantial, primeval clay, from which a coldness oozes, which will warp under your spade like chewing gum, bake solid in the sun and turn acid in the shade; a clay which is maleficent, unyielding, greasy and kiln-ready, as slippery as a snake and as dry as brick, as airtight as sheet metal and as heavy as lead. And now break it up with a pick, chop it with a spade, smash it with a hammer, turn it over and cultivate it, cursing loudly and lamenting. Then you will understand what enmity is and the obduracy of inanimate, sterile matter which ever did refuse to become a soil of life and still does now; and you will appreciate what a frightful struggle life must have engaged in, inch by inch, to take hold on the soil of the earth, whether that life be called vegetation or man.

And then you will also recognise that you have to give more to the soil than you take from it; you have to break it up and feed it with lime, and heat it with warm manure, sprinkle ashes on it lightly, and flood it with air and sunshine. Then the baked clay begins to fall apart and crumble as if it were breathing quietly; it yields loosely under your spade and with conspicuous willingness; it is warm and pliant in your palm; it is tamed. I tell you, to tame a few yards of soil is a great victory. Now it lies here, active, loose and warm. You would like to crumble all of it and rub it between your fingers to assure yourself of your victory. You do not even think about what you are going to sow in it now. What, is the sight of this dark, airy soil not beautiful enough? Is it not more beautiful than a bed of Pansies or a Carrot patch? You almost envy the vegetation which is going to take possession of this noble, human achievement called topsoil.

And from this time on you will not walk over the earth again not knowing what you are treading on. You will test every pile of earth and every bit of field in your palm and with your stick in the same way that another person might look at the stars, at people or at Violets; you will go into raptures over black topsoil, lovingly rub silky, forest leafmould, balance compact turf in your hand and weigh featherlight peat. 'Good Lord!' you will say, 'I'd like a truckful of this; and, damn it, a wagonful of this leafmould would do me some good; and this humus here, to sprinkle on top, and a couple of these cowpats here, and a pinch of this river sand, and a few barrowfuls of this rotten wood pulp, and a bit of this mud from the stream here, and these scrapings from the road wouldn't be bad, eh? And also the odd bit of phosphate and horn filings, but, heavens, this lovely, arable soil would do me too!' There are soils which are as fat as bacon, as light as a feather, as loose as cake, fair and black, dry and plumply soaked, which are all very varied and noble kinds of beauty; whereas ugly and contemptible is everything which is greasy, cloddish, wet, solid, cold, sterile and given to man to make him curse unredeemed matter; which is all just as ugly as the coldness, obduracy and malice of human souls.

Translated by Geoffrey Newsome

LIST OF ILLUSTRATIONS

ACKNOWLEDGMENTS

The publishers would like to thank Susannah Charlton, Publisher, RHS Books and Charlotte Brooks, Picture Librarian, RHS Lindley Library, for their help with this book.

The publishers would like to thank the following for permission to include in-copyright material:

The Medici Society for extract from *The Scented Garden* by Eleanour Sinclair Rohde; Curtis Brown Ltd on behalf of the author for extract from *The Well-Tempered Garden* by Christopher Lloyd (Penguin Books); Random House, Inc. and Penguin Books for extract from *Green Thoughts* by Eleanor Perényi; Curtis Brown Ltd on behalf of the author's estate for extract from *Some Ancient Gentleman* by Tyler Whittle (Heinemann); Farrar, Straus and Giroux, LLC and the executor of the author's estate for extract from *Onward and Upward in the Garden* by Katharine S. White; Random House, Inc. and The Society of Authors for extract from *The Education of a Gardener* by Russell Page; Grove/Atlantic, Inc and International Creative Management, Inc for extract from *Second Nature* by Michael Pollan; Chrysalis Books Group PLC for extract from *A Flower for Every Day* by Margery Fish (Batsford); Faber & Faber Ltd for extract from *Gardening Heresies and Devotions* by William Bowyer Honey; Curtis Brown Ltd on behalf of the author's estate for extract from *In Your Garden Again* by Vita Sackville-West (Frances Lincoln); Indiana University Press for 'Ode to the Toad' from *The Essential Earthman* by Henry Mitchell; Curtis Brown Ltd on behalf of the authors for extract from *Dear Friend and Gardener* by Beth Chatto and Christopher Lloyd (Frances Lincoln); Bloomsbury Publishing for extract from *The Tulip* by Anna Pavord; Timber Press for extract from *Garden Open Today* by Beverley Nichols; Continuum International Publishing Group Ltd, The Claridge Press and Geoffrey Newsome as translator for extract from *The Gardener's Year* by Karel Čapek.

The publishers apologise to any copyright holders that they were not able to trace and would like to hear from them.